NOT YET

WAYSON CHOY

NOT YET

A Memoir of Living and Almost Dying

DOUBLEDAY CANADA

Doubleday Canada and colophon are trademarks

Library and Archives Canada Cataloguing in Publication

Choy, Wayson, 1939–
Not yet / Wayson Choy.
ISBN 978-0-385-66310-6
1. Choy, Wayson, 1939- –Health. 2. Novelists, Canadian (English)–20th century–Biography. 3. Heart–Diseases–Patients–Canada–Biography. I. Title.
PS8555.H6658Z534 2009   c813'.54   C2008-906857-2
ISBN: 978-0-385-66310-6

Printed and bound in the USA

Published in Canada by Doubleday Canada,
a division of Random House of Canada Limited

Visit Random House of Canada Limited's website:
WWW.RANDOMHOUSE.CA

10 9 8 7 6 5 4 3 2 1

TO ALL WHO UNDERSTAND
LOVE HAS NO RULES.

Only in men's imagination does every truth find an effective and undeniable existence. Imagination, not invention, is the supreme master of art as of life.

Joseph Conrad, *A Personal Record*

AUTHOR'S NOTE

All memoirs are works of creative non-fiction, and this one is no exception. To protect the privacy of all hospital personnel and their patients and to respect the anonymity of some individuals, I have used fictitious names wherever necessary, and for narrative flow, I have collapsed chronologies and events.

Wayson Choy, Toronto 2008

Prologue

⁓

JUST AS I WAS TRUDGING DOWN THE STAIRS TO LEAVE FOR the Toronto airport, headed for Massachusetts, a sudden acidic tingling—a burning sensation—crept up from the back of my throat and triggered a hacking fit. My mouth contorted. My nostrils widened. My head whiplashed with the force of a hurricane; my mouth exploded in a sneeze. I snorted wetly like a cartoon pig. Gasping for air, I dug into my pocket for a tissue, and had anyone been there, I would have excused myself with, "Sorry. *Allergies.*"

My mind was too busy brooding over the deadline for my novel—the final deadline that would conclude three years of work. I had a month left to go.

As for the coughing, in the last two months or so I had fallen into fits of dry coughing, but if I held my breath, tightened my lungs, and didn't move a muscle for at least five seconds, I could breathe with ease again.

During July of 2001, with my book deadline looming, far from my mind was any thought that these spells could be signs of ill health, or worse. Only in Victorian dramas and novels, and in grand operas, does a cough or two foreshadow finis. Certainly, a sneeze lacks any hint of funereal dignity.

When I was young, I believed that I might die instantly, in a car crash or a great train wreck. In my late forties, I thought I might have a heart attack because I devoured too much fried meat and scorned leafy greens. By my fifties, I was waiting patiently for some dramatic sign of illness: cancer, for example, or a stroke, or AIDS, which had, by my sixth decade, taken away a dozen beloved friends.

But I remained lucky.

Now, in my sixties, and believing that I looked at least ten years younger, I had my mantra: whenever I coughed suddenly, coarsely, I told anyone nearby, "Sorry. *Allergies.*"

People nodded sympathetically. A few even said that they too swallowed little pills to numb their nasal passages. But by July my pills weren't working, and my extended family members, Karl and Marie, Jean and Gary, over a banquet dinner at the Pearl Court, said to me in chorus, "See your doctor!"

Two weeks before I left for my summer writing retreat in Massachusetts, I dutifully visited my doctor and friend, the man I called Dr. David.

Even after he told me, "You've had an asthmatic predisposition for most of your life, Wayson," I grumbled at the inconvenience of having so many damned allergies—to dust, pollen, cats, dogs, crabs, clams, oysters, smog.

David raised an eyebrow.

I did take care, I quickly clarified: we have a tabby, an aging cat named Belle, but I avoided petting her. Yes, my room was dusty, but only if I attempted to sweep did I suffer. I vacuumed every five years, religiously. I avoided certain kinds of shellfish, especially the kinds that I didn't like.

"And," I said, "I do have air conditioning in my third-floor space."

"Get a good air cleaner, too," David said. "Now that you're in your sixties, you're more vulnerable. You're asthmatic."

I blinked.

"Asthmatic?"

David patiently detailed in medical terms what that meant to me. He pointed to a set of bisected plastic lungs; his thoughtful demeanour suggested that he took me for one of his more intelligent patients, someone whose rapt Chinese-brown eyes actually glowed with understanding.

I smiled, I even nodded, as medical phrases sailed right past me.

David's concern for me, his youthful good looks and perfect office manners, charmed me, but from that meeting, I can only retrieve this fragment: "Yes, yes, Wayson, any one of your allergies can trigger a serious asthma attack."

Damn allergies, I told myself.

"Right after you come back from the States"—David tore off a prescription—"call me."

"Why?"

His hand gently gripped my shoulder. "I'm booking you to see a specialist."

"Oh," I said, appreciatively. "Well, give my regards to your wonderful wife and family."

As he does sometimes, David gave me a hug.

"You know," he said, walking me out to the reception area, "I've talked to a lot of people about some serious problems they're having, but, Wayson, you're the only one that stays smiling."

In the small waiting room, a few people looked up from the cushioned benches on each side of a burbling fish tank. On his mother's lap, a toddler banged together some alphabet blocks.

———

I was standing with my luggage at the top of our hall stairs. I couldn't wait any longer for Karl to assist me with my baggage: one bulging, scarred cowhide briefcase, one crammed-to-overflowing book tote, and my two seam-bursting suitcases.

The fifteen steps descending to our foyer might have discouraged a lesser man.

Think, I told myself, impatiently shuffling my feet.

A plan flashed in my head: I took a deep breath and lowered my left shoulder; next, my right one; looped the straps of each of the two smaller bags over them in turn, and stood up. The thick briefcase contained plastic Ziploc stacks of manuscript and research files, notebooks and index cards; the second, the oversized cloth bookbag printed with the face of Giller-winner Mordecai Richler, was stuffed with a collection of fountain pens, ballpoints, and pencils, rubber stamps of dragons and butterflies, erasers for ink and graphite, plus a brace of Chinese reference books. The two bags clunked against my hips like sacks of concrete. The belt-thick leather strap of the briefcase cut into my shoulder. Hands free, fingers ready to grasp the two suitcases, I stared down at the black-and-white-checkered hall below. I had forgotten to count the last footfall—the final touchdown onto the floor.

Sixteen steps.

All I had to do, I figured, was bend my knees a little, then grip the two suitcase handles, turn sideways, lift both cases, and negotiate the first step. I bent down, counted to three, and stood up. My shoulders and arms sagged with the weight of my favourite things: the big suitcase held the dictionary-sized reference books and more notebooks; six hundred manuscript pages; five files of research and clippings. The smaller suitcase contained my trusty laptop and portable printer with all its paraphernalia, plus enough clothes for two weeks.

My arms and legs went rubbery.

Didn't Karl say he would help me when he got back in from loading Marie's van? Didn't he say, "Wayson, I'll just be ten minutes"?

No. I can do this by myself.

I stiffened my back.

I can handle this.

My cough echoed down the staircase and through the empty house. The black-and-white floor tiles rose and fell in a wave. A meow rose from the kitchen below. Curious Belle trotted down the hall and sat by the bottom step, tabby tail flicking, to see what the madman from the attic was doing. I shrugged off the coughing. *Allergies.*

No time to waste. I gripped the suitcases and lifted them even higher. A gasp and half a cough escaped from me. I held my breath, tightened my lungs. The cough stopped.

With the baggage swaying about me, I turned sideways, and my foot landed on Step Two.

The damn cat has no deadlines to worry about.

My foot landed on Step Three, and a sudden sneeze threw me entirely off balance. The two suitcases banged against my legs. Briefcase and Mordecai Richler swung out. I began to pitch forward. But the weight of the briefcase swinging from my left side yanked me back against the railing. My body was bent at an angle.

Belle sat staring up at me.

I paused a few seconds to check for pain. Feeling none, I straightened up, too quickly. At once the shoulder strap on my briefcase began to slip down, freeing the bulk to arc away from me. The thing went flying, aiming on its return flight to smack the back of my knees and send me tumbling. Hissing through bared teeth, I twisted my head sideways, chomping my front ivories onto that tough strap of old leather. With clenched molars, adrenalin surging through me, I jerked the stiff loop back onto my shoulder. As the case swung back, I yanked the strap hard: the briefcase thumped safely to rest against my hip.

In my head, the trumpets of jubilation sounded: *I was still standing.*

My jaw aching, my neck throbbing, I thanked my stars that my front teeth, however imperfect, were my own. A pair of dentures would have spelled disaster.

On the other hand, no more book deadlines. *But everything else to lose,* I thought, and quickly added, *No, not yet.*

ONE

Marschallin to Octavian:

"One must take things lightly, with light heart and light hands hold and take, hold and relinquish . . ."

—Richard Strauss, *Der Rosenkavalier*

Chapter 1

⁓

FLAT ON MY BACK, I TRIED TO OPEN MY EYES.

Nothing.

Still alive, I thought.

I remembered a long needle pointed towards me, and a doctor, his masked face bending over me, his steady voice both encouraging and oddly routine, saying, *Now, please count slowly backwards from one hundred*; and my own voice faintly responding, *Ninety-nine, ninety-eight* . . . when a veil of sleep fell over me. The rhythm of sounds drifted in and out of my consciousness: beeping machinery tangled with fragments of casual talk, medical phrases, numbers.

For however long I was sedated, I felt only a semblance of discomfort but no pain. Eventually, I tried to open my eyes to catch sight of the person whose fingers were massaging me towards wakefulness.

Don't stop, I tried to say. I struggled to pronounce a salutation remembered from my Chinatown childhood, *Ten thousand blessings from my ancestors to yours!*

If I found the individual rubbing my forehead to be someone unknown to me, I might even lift my eyebrow, and whisper something about the kindness of strangers. But, unable to move so much as an eyelid, I simply lay there, aware that my life had been saved.

Alive, I thought.

I did not know how long I had been out. Too weak even to ask for water, I did manage to press my tongue against my teeth, but felt only grit and the curving shape of the tube stuck down my throat.

I tried again to speak, to signal that I was aware of the fingers brushing back my hair, but my lips refused even to twitch. Efforts to mumble, *Thank you, thank you,* dissolved into quiet gurgling in my chest. *Sorry,* I thought, *I can't seem to move.*

The warm hand touching me sensed my frustration; the palm and fingers fell into a caressing motion, as if to chase away the thick fog in my head. All I knew for sure was that I was still in a hospital, caught in a catastrophe, and that someone was standing by me. Yet voices faintly echoed from my past, the nagging warnings of my parents and the elders of Chinatown, their fears for my bachelor ways singsonged back into my drugged head like a chorus from an ancient opera.

One day you be old and sick and no wife be there for you, the voices scolded. *For sure, you marry or no one be with you!*

No son!

No daughter!

You die alone!

The voices had not stopped until, at twenty-three, I did what many young people did then, and still do, consciously or not—I left home to begin a life where I could discover my own values. Freshly graduated from UBC, and inspired by the speeches of Martin Luther King Jr., I went east in 1962 on a civil rights protest, hitchhiking to Ottawa to demand that Prime Minister Lester B. Pearson protect the rights of all citizens equally, regardless of race. Forty years on, here I was, still single, still in Toronto, immobilized on a bed in St. Michael's hospital.

But someone cared enough to stay with me.

I'm not forgotten, I thought. *I'm not alone.*

With a soft tissue, the same hand blotted the corner of my eyes, a gesture so intimate, so sure, that it wiped away the ancient voices.

When I finally stirred awake again, struggling against the effects of the anaesthesia, the soothing hand was gone. My eyes remained shut; they would not open. *Is anyone there?* I heard soft beep-beep sounds from the machinery keeping watch over the push-pull of my asthmatic lungs. Attempting to raise my head and failing, I felt the ticking of my bachelor heart. *Where is everyone?* I tried to move, but could not turn my head or even lift a finger. I tried to press my dry tongue against the roof of my mouth. A tube was still in the way. The air tasted of disinfectant. I could feel and hear people around me but could not see.

"I need to clamp and adjust," a male voice was saying. "Move the lamp here."

The light above me brightened; the orange haze pressing through my eyelids turned into a surreal vision of pink and red veins. Unable to call out or grip someone's hand, I felt helpless. This same helplessness had swallowed me when I saw first my mother, and then five years later, my father pass quietly away in their hospital rooms. Perhaps the voices of Chinatown were right: Why would anyone be there for you unless they were blood-bound?

Do you think you so special?

What do you expect?

Against a rising sense of dread, and against a tide of self-pity, I pushed myself to play out a favourite childhood game. The game had been impressed into my boyhood life during those war years when Japan invaded China and Vancouver's rooming houses were suddenly filled with news from the old country: I would be a righteous, brave soldier. I would withstand the worst. The luminous tracery of red and pink veins dissolved into darkness and turned into fluttering banners.

At first, I couldn't remember clearly how I got into this situation, lying in a bed in the intensive care unit, battling for my life. Much later, as the medicines were being withdrawn, I would remember the severe asthma attack that had tightened my chest the humid August night I had returned from my writing retreat.

I would remember how, instead of dealing with my symptoms, I had complained to my worried housemates about Toronto's polluted air; as for my cough, I dismissed it with my standard theory about summer colds. Allergies. A little rest will cure anything.

Marie interrupted me. "Wayson, your breathing doesn't sound right."

"Listen to yourself," Karl said, and mimicked my rasping to demonstrate the obvious.

"I'm scheduled to give a keynote speech tomorrow," I reminded them. I took a deep breath and stared them down, the two of them, sealing my fate. "Thanks for the concern," I said, surprised to be speaking so abruptly, "but three hundred educators will be there."

I stormed up the two flights of stairs and, shaking and exhausted, went straight to bed.

Instead of falling into a restful sleep, I lay half awake, tossing and hacking. At one-thirty in the morning, spasms in my throat jolted me awake. I hacked and gasped for oxygen. Fortunately, a rush of adrenalin chased away my light-headedness and shook me alert. Clarity hit me: my lungs were failing fast; they were shuddering into paralysis. Collapsing. I kicked away the bedding, fumbled about for pants and shirt. My chest tightened: the membranes were swelling, the air passages narrowing. I coughed so hard in the struggle for air that I was thrown against the wall.

I frantically tucked in my shirt, zipped up, and stumbled down the narrow third-floor steps to slump against Karl and Marie's bedroom door.

"Can't breathe," I croaked. "Going to emergency."

Karl's voice thundered: "Don't move!"

"We'll drive you," Marie shouted.

I leaned against the wall, stubbornly ready to drive myself. I searched my pocket for my car keys. The bedroom door flew open, the two of them throwing on clothes as they rushed me down the last staircase and out the front door into the rain-damp night. Karl unlocked his car and started the engine. Marie guided me into the passenger seat and shut the door. She sat in the back, asked if I was belted in. Karl reached over. I heard the mechanism click.

As we drove through the empty streets, I felt a sudden calm and focused my eyes on Karl's profile. A gentle rain began to fall, refracting the light into droplets that ran down his cheeks. I first encountered that handsome face when he was nineteen and shyly ambled into my Literature and Psychology class, all six-foot-two of him, fresh from the farming village of Creemore. By the end of that first semester, he proved to be a brilliant student, and he even thought of becoming a writer. Much later, we bonded. I held his hand to thank him for some carpentry work he had done for me at my house. Given that he was straight, he let my hand linger upon his much longer than I dared to expect. He had been warned by some of his well-meaning friends to be careful of fags like me. He didn't pay much attention to them; he was his own man. Simply put, he liked me. Later, he showed me some of his writing. I became his mentor, his friend.

I saw Karl struggle through two or three relationships in the years that followed. I bluntly told him to leave Marie—the very last one that stole his heart. The woman couldn't make up her mind to move in with him or to quit him. I was on vacation in B.C. when he phoned for my advice. The situation didn't sound very promising to me: after all, she was in the fashion business.

"Give her a real consequence," I said.

Two thousand miles away, it was easy for me to be callous. Didn't she understand what a decent and open-hearted man he was? Green-eyed jealousy gripped me: *Why can't he be mine?*

"Let her know if she moves out again, it's over. Karl, just forget her!" My tone turned righteous and cold. "The truth is, she doesn't appreciate you."

He told Marie what I had said. She demanded to meet the busybody.

When I returned to Toronto, Marie and I agreed to meet without Karl, on some neutral territory, ready to do battle. I reserved a table at a Mexican-style restaurant at Carlton and Parliament. She came up and introduced herself, a tall, beautiful woman, perfectly made up, her eyes glinting back the candle-lit room.

She sat down, stared hard at me for minutes on end while I talked about how lucky she was to have Karl be so in love with her. I left behind my jealousy after the first five minutes, and my words went flying out on their own, shamelessly extolling his virtues.

"He's one of the finest and kindest men I have ever met," I concluded.

Marie never once interrupted me. Now, she put down her glass of wine, took my measure. Her eyes softened.

"You love him, too," she said. "He must be worth it."

The next day I told Karl not to lose her. "She's sane," I said. "She appreciates you."

And me, I thought.

In the months that followed, the three of us hung out together. We dined on my soy-marinated pork chops, crunched on her fresh salads, and laughed at Karl's jokes; it dawned on each of us that we three might even buy a house together. The next summer, as house prices and rents rose, and every downtown Toronto property had half a dozen frantic buyers bidding, Marie and I found a house we liked—"It feels like a lucky house," we instantly told each other—and the three of us bought it.

The next year, my eighty-four-year-old father, dying of cancer, came to live with us in our fixer-upper semi-detached home on Saulter Street, just around the dingy corner from the Hells Angels' walled compound. Immediately, Karl renovated a room and put in a bathroom for my father. With Marie expecting a child, they decided to get married. Before my father left Toronto to finish his days in Vancouver, I took a snapshot of him, grinning happily, holding baby Kate, my goddaughter, in his arms. Just before my father left for Vancouver, the house indeed proved lucky: a lottery ticket I bought won a prize of $100,000.

Now, twenty years later, living in a bigger house in Riverdale, the four of us were still together. Kate was in Montreal checking out residences at McGill University. And on this warm August evening, in 2001, Karl and Marie and I were speeding through the wet Toronto night. Between my heaving and gasping, with Marie's hand on my shoulder to steady me as the car whipped around corners, I heard the wheels spinning in the rain.

We lurched to a stop right in front of the sliding doors marked For Emergency Only. Karl unbelted me, reached over to open the passenger door. Gripping my arm with both her hands, Marie guided me into the brightly lit waiting room.

Hours later, as the sun was rising, a young doctor explained to Karl and Marie how the medicines he had administered to their friend during the last six hours were not working.

"He's in pretty bad shape." The doctor looked to see that I, lying in my hospital gown on the gurney, also understood what was going on. "Acute respiratory distress syndrome."

"Failing lungs," I managed to say. I tried to laugh, but wheezed instead.

The nurse handed me a surgical consent form to sign. Another nurse prepared a syringe. Karl and Marie stepped aside. No one was smiling. An orderly waited beside the gurney for the signal to transfer me to the intensive care unit. The pen wandered across the signature line.

"We'll have to intubate you," the doctor explained, looking steadily at me. "Slip a tube inside your airway. You'll be very heavily sedated until your lungs recover."

"How long will that take?" Marie asked.

"On average? If nothing else goes wrong, we don't like going beyond three days." He turned to me: "Are you fine with that?"

I nodded and studied grim-faced Karl, then Marie, and now my close friend Mary Jo, summoned at my request. I wiped the side of my mouth with the back of my hand and attempted to take in a full breath.

"I want you to know"—I managed half a breath—"I love you all very much."

Mary Jo frowned. "We don't need to know that right now."

"Well," I gasped, "just in case."

I raised my head, anxious to remind Karl that I was scheduled to give a keynote speech in the morning. *Did I bring my summer-weight blazer? A fresh shirt?*

"Don't worry," he said.

"Let's go," the doctor said, and the nurse stepped up with a long syringe. "Mr. Choy, this will make things easier."

Seconds before the needle slipped in, I heard the young doctor say, "We'll be doing everything we can for you."

Thank you, I wanted to say. Instead, I had only a second to feel disconcerted by all this unnecessary attention.

Someone pushed a pillow under my head.

I closed my eyes to the squeaking of the metal gurney wheeling me away. The squeaks turned into my mother's voice. I was five years old again, being prepared by a medical team to have my tonsils removed; Mother cried out in her Toishanese, *Now, now, just you be brave soldier.* And before the potent drug knocked my brain out, my mother's gentle face burst into tears.

⁓

After days sunk in a fog of darkness, the brave soldier awoke. For the second or third time—or maybe the tenth—I struggled to stay alert, and each time I regained some consciousness I found myself attached to more monitoring machines, taped with more electrodes and more dripping tubes. Most of the time, I could see nothing; other times, I glimpsed smears of images, misshapen heads and torsos and elongated hands moving above and around me.

"Nice to see you awake, Mr. Choy," a nurse said to me each time I stirred in confusion or opened my eyes in panic and attempted to talk or swallow. Then a quick explanation would follow: a tube—a sturdy device—had been eased down my throat to inflate and bathe my lungs with oxygen.

"Don't try to talk," the woman said. "You won't feel the tube after a few minutes. Get some rest, Mr. Choy."

And then I would sink into darkness, comforted by the sound of pulsing. I heard snippets of conversation between Marie and the doctors. My country family, Gary and Jean, were there, too. Gary called out my name. After a few seconds, Jean murmured a few words—*Oh, Wayson, Wayson*—and broke down.

Someone else had arrived. I tried to flex my elbows to raise myself up to greet the person, but my elbows wouldn't move. I tried turning my head. Useless. My arms and legs felt hollow, empty of sinew and muscle.

Can't even lift a finger.

I lay like a mannequin, its stiff neoprene skull exposed and stuffed with questions: *Did I say thank you? Am I wearing my new shirt? Is my hair combed?* Then the life-saving monitors would hiss and pump, click and beep, and I would focus again on my own tenuous mortality.

Insane, I thought. *I'm dying and worried about my hair.*

During certain moments of my nearly eleven days and nights of induced sedation, sensible questions threaded in and out of my wakefulness: How long had I been lying here? How many days had I lost? How many hours had I been falling into half-dreams that ballooned into cartoon nightmares? Not only had everyday reality slipped away from my consciousness but time had also been vanquished.

I stood before the towering Gates of Life, looked up at a huge stone temple, its giant pillars carved with fire-breathing serpents, creatures resurrected from the stories spun by Chinatown elders. Beside me, grinning skull-faced Death stood, my wrist gripped tightly ringed by his bony fingers, intending to drag me into his embrace. Somehow, I snatched my hand away and escaped.

Am I afraid of dying?

No, I responded, surprising myself. *No I am not.*

Instead of shaking like the Cowardly Lion, I envisioned my fists clenched high like kung-fu clubs, my face as fierce as a Cantonese opera warrior's, a brazen soldier fully armed, too proud to beg even at the Gates of Life.

My brain cells flickered, fireflies in the deepening night. Voices called out to me: a nurse or doctor gave me instructions to lift my arm, to grunt, to nod my head; a familiar voice told me of news from the world outside. I felt the strongest urge to get up and go home, to simply stand up and rip away the intravenous tubes, tear away the EKG wires, and pull free of the catheter tethering me to the bed.

How difficult could that be?

I attempted to swallow. I gagged. I tried to shove my tongue against the tubing. I opened my mouth as wide as I could, hacking from the very back of my throat to eject the obstacle. I sat up. The machine's beeps became more insistent.

"Restrain him," a voice cried.

Strong hands forced me back. Straps were tugged. Pulled. Pushed and locked. Needles, syringes, prodded and poked. Tubes and catheters were adjusted. The ventilator pumped and pushed. Stronger sedatives began to take effect. The urge in me to move and push things away collapsed. Fiery serpents, towering gates, flew away. I descended into a smouldering darkness.

"What are his chances, Doctor?"

"Fifty-fifty."

Distantly, people walked away from my bed. The few atoms left of me slept.

Chapter 2

⟋

LONG AFTERWARDS, WHEN I WANTED TO TRACK WHAT had happened during that first week of my medical crisis, I requested copies of my charts from St. Michael's Hospital. The records revealed not only that I had endured a severe asthma attack but that I had also suffered "multiple cardiac events."

In order to intubate me, the ICU team had put me in a state of what is called induced unconsciousness, so I wouldn't choke when the tube was inserted.

To guard against stroke-like injuries to my brain, I was kept under semi-sedation. A young intern assigned watch would ask me questions to monitor my perilous state.

"Can you hear me, Mr. Choy?"

I managed to nod. Barely.

Depending upon the half dozen opiates and chemicals dripped or injected into my veins, I slipped back and forth between semi-consciousness and waves of deep narcotic sleep. It was a delicate job, keeping a sixty-two-year-old asthmatic in a healing sedation, a calming stupor only a layer or two above the boundaries of a deadly coma.

Some years later, when I interviewed the young doctor—Dr. Steve—in St. Mike's cafeteria during his lunch break, he recalled how he smiled when I responded to his questions, especially if I nodded and gripped his extended fingers, however feebly.

"After the third day," he said, "there can be a real danger of a brain trauma."

My lungs were still weak, but by the third day they seemed to be improving. Dr. Steve remembered how the team cheered up a bit.

Then things got interesting. Calendar and clock time disappeared. Suffering from ICU psychosis, I began to hallucinate. Someone was stealing glasses of water from me; a black dog with yellow eyes lumbered up to slather my hand with its thick tongue. Nagging thoughts bounced about and slithered down a glass bowl smeared with Vaseline: *Hadn't I signed a contract to go to China to make a film about Confucius?*

Yes, you did sign up, Confucius answered, in perfect English, and then his ancient face vanished.

And then another question shot up: *Didn't I have a dinner date?*

A forkful of savoury prime beef touched my tongue. I could taste the saltiness but not swallow.

I opened my eyes. Through a haze of yellow fog, I tried to find Marie but could only make out shadowy clumps that shifted whenever I moved my head. I wondered where she and Mary Jo had gone. I tried to call out for Karl to drive me home. But my throat muscles merely tightened around the thick ventilator tube. No sound left me.

No one answered.

The machinery around me beep-beeped away. Unable to completely open up my eyes and blink away the haziness, I tried to raise my fingers, to gesture for assistance. I attempted to raise my arm, to shift my legs. My limbs refused to move.

Why not let go? Sink away?

The chemicals coursing through my veins began to dissolve my wakefulness. Eyelids folded shut. My jaw slackened. As I slipped away, I heard someone say, *Mr. Choy, can you hear me?*

After a timeless absence, a quick movement—a shuffling against the mattress—stirred me awake. Through amplified lashes, like a squinting alien, I glimpsed Jean and Gary. They were standing beside me, huddled together, Jean in tears. Gentle, bearded Gary held on to her. Gary reached out and touched my forehead.

I was not alone!

Family's here, I thought, and suddenly an expanse of bright green lawn opened up before my mind's eye, sweeping me back thirty-six years. I am waiting for Gary's approach. He strides towards where I am sitting; he is twenty-five once more, tanned and limber, looking rugged in his army shorts. His craggy face, his beard, remind me of a marauding Viking. *Someone's lucky catch,* I think. He cheerfully accepts the invitation from the principal to grab one of the lawn chairs and joins us.

"How's the hunting this season, Gary?" the principal asks.

"Fine," he answers. "But my army training comes first this summer."

Turned out he was in the reserves, a lieutenant with the Grey and Simcoe Foresters, a regiment in the Armoured Corps. I wondered what he thought of pacifists like me.

The white-haired principal had been interviewing me for a teaching position. In fact, because I had a degree and Gary hadn't completed his, I was being interviewed to take over Gary's job. I had not been warned about this awkward situation. After all, it was none of my business. I had come to the village of Durham to escape the stresses of my recent promotion at MacLaren's: success at a big Toronto ad agency was no longer fun or satisfying.

At the principal's request, Gary asked me a few questions to expose my instincts as an untested teacher of English. The man's rough veneer hid his softer side: he cared for his students.

" . . . and that's how I might teach Steinbeck," I concluded. "Tell them enough of the story to hook them into reading the book."

He must have liked what he heard. He went directly home and told Jean, "Pack up. We're leaving."

He didn't lose this job. At the last minute, the board got approval to start up a Commercial program. They renewed Gary's contract.

In Toronto, two weeks before school was set to start, I received a phone call. Gary wondered if I had a place to live in Durham. I hadn't even thought of packing. Would I like to board with his family?

"I have two kids," he warned me, "ages three and four. They're a bit, well, rambunctious. Can you live with—?"

"The rent," I said. "How much is the rent?"

I figured the first month would allow me enough time to find a private place of my own. How long could one cope with two toddlers? He mentioned an absurdly low figure, unheard of in Toronto. The sum included a bedroom with a weekly change of linen, all utilities, a shared office, use of the kitchen and living room—plus, *if I didn't mind*—Jean's cooking.

"I'll take it."

"But the kids can be pretty hectic, maybe you'd—"

"No, that's okay," I said. "You should know, though, I'm a pacifist."

"Are you religious about that?"

"No, but I work with the Quakers on civil rights issues. Can you tolerate that?"

"Hey, if you can live with my two kids, why not?"

By my second year of living with them, I was named godfather to their children, Tosh and Gary Jr. In kindergarten, Gary Jr. blurted out his catalogue of family members: "I got a sister, a mommy and daddy, and a Wayson."

Befitting a gay godfather free to roam, I gave them brush-painting lessons, *Alligator Pie*, noise-making toy pianos and drums, spoiled them with attendance at circuses and festivals, and encouraged them to memorize a line or two from Shakespeare. By their teen years, I gave up trying to find a place of my own.

Listen, I told all those righteous voices that had warned me of a dire bachelorhood, *I am not alone.*

Peering up at Jean and Gary, my spirit lifted with the thought: *I've never been alone.* As I glimpsed them between my lashes, the opiates floated me away. Now, the two would see only the whites of my eyes, as if I were dead; observe a thick tube curving out from a swollen mouth; they would notice the shunts taped to my wrists, and look with disbelieving eyes at the tangle of syringes and transfusion lines, and they would weep.

Awake. I felt strangely afloat. No clock hung on the hospital wall that I could see. The lights were on. Disinfectant tickled my nose. *Was it now midnight or high noon? How many days had slipped by? Where had everyone gone?*

The towering gates had long vanished. I was awake, gazing out openly, seeing things clearly again. I stared at the globed lights and the white hospital ceiling and felt alert, on guard, but not like any child soldier. It came to me that I was sixty-two— and wasn't I a writer? Some odd energy hummed inside me. Voices crisscrossed my wakefulness.

Hang on

Seize the moment!

You're having an adventure!

Familiar voices chimed in again: *The signs! Pay attention to the signs!*

Long ago, Chinatown elders had taught me about signs. From the age of three, I knew that good little boys who survived the attack of the sharp-toothed, lip-smacking Fox Lady always stood on guard for the clues that would betray her evil intentions. Though her shape changed into the guise of an old lady, the Demon Fox could not hide her thick tail. Whenever she was about to devour her young prey, her furry tail wagged eagerly beneath her skirt.

I paid attention: a part of my brain had awakened, lucid and independent of drugs and sleep and sickness, and acknowledged that all the monitors and catheters were, probably, signs.

Was I dying? Was I afraid?

I told myself: *Not possible.*

In my twenties, I had convinced myself that I would never be afraid of dying, never be afraid of that euphemistic "last stage of growth." And I accepted that my dying would be inevitable— like everyone else's—but mine would be entirely without pain.

A painless death had always seemed to me a sensible prospect. I had never considered enduring *any* physical pain whatsoever.

My fingers turned phantom notebook pages, and my right hand began twitching, as if I were writing down my Rules of Dying:

One: Note all signs, to prevent surprises.

Two: Never perish in a garret. If you're to swan away, choose a five-star location or the best hospice.

Three: Avoid pain at all costs. If any artistic sacrifice exacts physical pain, do something else less annoying.

Sedation greatly assisted my adherence to these rules, especially the third one. In fact, there *was* pain. A great deal of exhausting pain. I was simply too drugged-up to notice, too busily distracted by my phantom writing. I felt none of the lightning now beginning to strike at my struggling heart and failing lungs, which the monitors recorded.

I lay calmly, even when there appeared, right behind the glowing outlines of the medical team working over me, a gaunt, hooded rider astride a moon-pale horse. The skeletal rider boldly stood up on silver stirrups, crooked his bony index finger to bid me: *Mount!*

The ghostly sight startled me, but then my literary instincts twigged to it all: *Aha! The classic symbol for Cervantes' Father Death—* "I see a Pale Horse, Pale Rider," cried madly sane Don Quixote, "and he bids me, 'Mount!'"

Identified, horse and rider vanished. But my mind played on: *Would there be other signs? Would there suddenly appear a vista of a sunset grander than I could ever imagine?* My ears pricked up at the sound of Chinese string instruments, their half-tone cries whining through crashing cymbals and thundering drums. Then a Heavenly Choir began to belt out a climactic *Alleluia!*

Crisp voices interrupted. The music stopped. A medical instrument jolted my elbow.

"Increasing the dosage?"

"Yes," someone answered. "One fifty."

"He's very resistant."

I am, I thought. *You're holding back the Heavenly Choir.*

The steady ding-ding-dinging of the ventilator and the beep-beep-beeping of the cardiac monitor jumped into my hearing. *Alarms.* I found the strength to push someone aside. I fought to sit up.

As the medical team shuffled around me, someone ordered the bright lamps to be raised. Someone else shouted for assistance to hold me down. How odd. As the lamps were raised, the light grew darker. Fatigue swamped me. As my mind sailed into emptiness, my brain rattled on: *Is this dying? Could I be dying now? No sunset vista? No music?*

My clutching fingers scribbled into the air a brief comment: *Dying—is—boring.*

One night in the ICU—was it the third or fourth?—countless distraught faces hovered over me. I remember catching snatches of whispering, of someone sniffling, and of another crying out, "My God, he looks terrible."

"Don't you die," a woman's voice said. "Don't you dare!"

When I could open my eyes—or thought I opened my eyes—no one was there. Someone called out my name.

I'm here!

I saw myself leaping from the bed, storming out of the ward. *Where are my clothes?* I desperately wanted to yank out the tube in my mouth. Thirst tightened my throat. Without warning, a cloudburst broke over my head; raindrops pelted down. Every liquid drop splashed down in slow, agonizing motion, and every single drop missed my open mouth and turned into droplets of perspiration sliding down my cheeks.

The heat rising from my body seemed to be coming from the tube in my throat. Deep in my lungs, it had somehow caught on fire and was incinerating my insides. I felt my heart slamming against its cage, trying to escape the flames.

A palm touched my forehead. I heard voices but couldn't make out what was being said.

Let me be, I pleaded. *Let me go.*

The flames died out. I sank into a half-wakeful state again. I could not move, but was no longer panicked. My mind recreated the first time that I wished this deeply to be dead.

It happened in Grade Seven. Fresh from studying a poem by Dylan Thomas, I read aloud my first two-page story composition to the class. My story's young hero died rescuing his dog, and I wrote, "The boy sank his tired teeth into that final good night."

The teacher and the whole class roared with laughter.

"I didn't mean it to be funny," I said, which doubled the volume of catcalls and guffaws.

I sat down. I couldn't keep from blushing. If I could stop my heart cold, or at least starve it of oxygen, it would stop pumping blood into my cheeks. I held my breath.

My heart didn't stop beating. Now it pounded loudly in my ears. My tongue felt hot. My mouth burned with heat. Flames flared inside my lungs.

"Nurse," someone called, "increase the dosage."

At the same moment as someone held up my wrist to inject the dose, a gloved hand gently opened my mouth, and a quenching liquid spray coated my mouth and tongue. I eased into a slow tranquility. I heard the monitor next to me pulsing steadily.

"Close call, Mr. Choy," a voice said. "Can you hear me?"

Chapter 3

IN MY DRUGGED CONDITION, DURING THAT FIRST WEEK, time, like a Dali watch, melted. And yet throughout that period, keenly felt incidents imprinted themselves onto my semi-comatose mind. I sometimes shifted restlessly, then hardly moved at all. Lying perfectly still, I could hear the medical staff working over me.

"Vitals steady?"

"Okay here."

"Everyone ready?"

I felt a palm lightly tap my chest. Someone else tugged at the thick tube lodged in my throat.

"Disconnect, please."

The beeping pattern changed. The clicking of another machine registered in my ears. A pressure ballooned within my rib cage, and heat again seared my throat. Slowly, the ventilator tube began its forward slide. I choked. My heart thumped. The beeping went mad.

"Call the cardiologist."

Floating above, I saw someone rush to the bed. Transfixed with double vision, seeing from above and below at the same time, I caught the doctor's frown, the look of shock when she caught me staring back at her, wide-eyed.

"Problem," she said. "Check . . ."

Numbers were called out. Faces loomed over me. Monitors chirped like crazed cicadas. The tube continued to slither in my throat as my muscles fought back. I gagged. My heart boomed. Firm hands grabbed at my flailing arms.

"Code Blue!"

Cool, I thought as I took in the action. *They actually say Code Blue.*

Someone swabbed my body. I glimpsed masked faces, and probing eyes stared back. Across the landscape of my body, instruments, intravenous lines and tubes abounded.

"Dosage?"

"Seventy-five."

A wave of warmth and then a pool of calm opened inside me. *Enough,* I thought, and let go.

After, as before, bits of news filtered in. Friends and colleagues came and talked about the college, laughed at jokes I couldn't catch. Countless times I heard, "Wayson, you're getting better" and "People are asking about you"—and as many times, "Wayson, if you can hear me, please nod." My vision badly blurred by drugs, I could barely make out who spoke, barely recall their whispered names.

Someone wiped the drool from my face.

"Wake up, sir."

My eyes, much to my surprise, opened wide. Two young men, one wearing a green and the other a red shirt of similar cut—orderlies, I thought—stood smiling beside a much older woman, a nurse in a starched white uniform. She checked the name on my wrist band.

"Mr. Choy?"

I nodded, a little groggy.

"These two gentlemen are going to rub your body," the nurse said matter-of-factly. "Doctor's orders. A massage will help prevent bedsores and blood clots."

Just in case I might be one of those old guys who would resist a doctor's order, two handsome faces looked back at me with encouragement. Did they guess how lucky I felt at that moment, waking up to their smiles? The blond one gestured to let me know he was going to slip another pillow under my head. Then he untied my gown at the neck. The nurse took the garment away. With some terror that my old flesh and bones might dishearten, even disgust, them, I sank back, exposed but for a modest towel draped below my waist.

Without a pause, Blondie stepped behind my head, extended his arms, and began working on my shoulders. They creaked.

The dark-haired one, looking no more than twenty-five, kept himself busy taping down the shunts with a film of protective plastic and lifting cords off me. Satisfied that he could work without any serious hindrance, he rolled up his red sleeves and began to massage my wrists and arms. His dark hair fell over his blue eyes. His thin lips barely curved when he smiled. I definitely know him, had seen him somewhere. With that hank of boyish hair falling over those intense eyes, he could have been a movie star. He caught me staring; he smiled back. I feigned indifference. The two went ahead with the doctor's order, like two oarsmen. Coolly professional. Four strong hands subtly sensed how gently palms might rub, how firmly fingers grip and knuckles press. In rhythm to their push-pull strokes, I inhaled. I felt a kind of happiness, to be touched without judgement, without shame or disgust.

I exhaled.

Pleasure overwhelmed me: I could feel a familiar growing warmth in my groin, the towel tenting, as if I were sixteen instead of sixty-two. Neither one seemed to take much notice, or at least seemed to care. I was revived by their efforts to save me from bedsores and blood clots, an effort lasting no more than a few minutes and forever, and they seemed to communicate their permission for me to indulge in whatever fantasy I cared to have.

Now, standing on opposite sides of me, they efficiently nudged my flesh and pulled at the joints of my fingers, gradually moving down my torso, their oiled palms and fingers sliding down to my calves and feet. When they reached the soles of my feet, a spectacular groan escaped from me. The whites of my eyes must have rolled to the back of my head. They retreated.

Massage, finis.

Efficient as clockwork, the nurse appeared, slipped a gown on me, unfolded a bedsheet from my feet to my chin, leaving me just as I was before. The blond lifted my head and took away the second pillow. With a nod to his partner, he turned to leave.

I couldn't help staring at the dark-haired one in that red shirt. It seemed he could read my mind. He came back, rested his hand on my arm. "I'll see you again," he said.

Where were you, I wanted to ask, *when I was as young as you, craving to be noticed?*

As he hurried to catch up to his colleague, the nurse said to me, "You will see him again, Mr. Choy." She sounded definite. "He'll come back when you need him. It's doctor's orders."

I closed my eyes and fragments of nursing talk rolled by me again like waves. Gradually, even the clink of medical tools, submitted to the hospital's silence. There was only the steady beeping of monitors, like so many crickets at peace with the night.

A voice burst loudly at me, as if from a megaphone: "Mr. Choy, please count from ten—backwards—just to yourself. Can you do that?"

My throat was dry. I smelled the same familiar blanket covering me. I had not been moved or touched. Or massaged by anyone. Phantoms had come into the room, and as the request was repeated directly in my ear—*eight . . . six . . . three*—a movie screen stretched across the ceiling.

I am sixteen. I have arrived late at the movie house. As I hurry to find the aisle seat my best friend, Philip, has saved for me, I watch the screen, mesmerized, unable to take my eyes away. A slim young man is running down a street. The music is frantic, primal, suggesting a breathless life-and-death chase. In a close-up on that gigantic screen, I see a hank of brown hair bounce over steel eyes. And I am sixteen again, saying to myself, *I will never forget you, James Dean, running in your red windbreaker, breaking my heart, forever.*

When I woke up, I found I was still breathing. Even more surprising, I felt an enormous rough tongue licking my hand and caught a dank scent.

I turned my head and saw a thick-headed, friendly black Labrador. The overhead lights were clearly reflected in its large eyes. Its blunt nose damply nudged my wrist. I looked up at the dog's owner. The young woman hesitated, about to smile or speak. Her thin lips moved, but no sound came out. I frowned, remembering I was lying in a hospital bed. *What was this dog doing here?* No beast, however friendly, should be leaving slime on my hand.

The animal's rough tongue lapped at my wrist again. The woman jerked the dog's leash, and the thick-boned head was yanked back. Choking with anger, and unable to shout out my protest, I punched my fist in the air. The dog looked at me, puzzled.

The beeping went mad. I fought to get up, to chase away the woman. A blurred mob of white masks appeared; hands pinned down my legs and arms.

"Wayson, can you hear me?" a new voice asked. The others fell silent. From the sudden hush, I heard: "You have to settle down." It was a comforting voice, a woman's voice. "You have to calm down. I'm here now to watch over you."

I could open my eyes, and did. A gentle face hovered over me. The black dog was gone.

"See? It's me."

I blinked away the haziness.

"It's Tosh," she said.

As I tried to raise my arms to embrace her, my goddaughter's smile distracted me from the fact that my body was now strapped down. At that moment, I would not have cared even if my limbs had been amputated.

"Wayson," Tosh repeated, "I'm here."

Within me, the ancient voices of the elders were dumbstruck.

Chapter 4

"IT'S MICHAEL, MR. CHOY," A YOUNGER VOICE SAID. "I'M going to be with you for a few days, take care of you."

I nodded.

"Can you feel this?" Firm fingers gently kneaded my jaw open. With a wet tissue, Michael moistened and wiped the inside of my mouth. He rubbed my teeth and gums. My mouth tingled with the taste of mint. As he closed my mouth, I pressed my tongue against a liquid-laden swab that seemed to burst like a cold fountain onto the back of my throat. I opened my eyes wide, seeking another.

"Mike—Michael?"

I saw the living head of Michelangelo's *David* smile at me. I garbled his creator's name.

He laughed. "No, no, I'm just called Michael," he said. "I'm your nurse."

A fresh bedsheet covered me.

Michael stood silently beside my bed. Tosh stood on the other side, holding my hand.

"Hello, Wayson," she said. "I'm still here."

Comforted, I fell asleep.

⌒

No more metal parts pressed against my body. That was the first thing I noticed when I woke up.

"We're moving you to the recovery ward because you're stronger now. Is that okay with you, Mr. Choy?" Michael asked.

Something was said about the ventilator, the tube, something about the thin line of oxygen being clipped to my nostrils. I made an effort to talk, but could only nod.

Two other figures appeared. I felt more movement. Clinking sounds rose and fell. A nurse adjusted the flexible tubes lying across my chest. Sturdy palms braced my neck; strong arms slid under my back, and another slipped under the crook of my knees.

"At three," Michael said. "One, two . . . three!"

My arms and palms stiffened. I floated up. When I landed on the metal gurney, the contraption shook. A tiny pillow under my left arm balanced an array of taped intravenous lines. Another count of three and I rose in the air again, landing with ease on a firm mattress.

Wanting to savour the linen-fresh, sugary crispness wafting from the sheets and new pillows, I tightened my windpipe and inhaled. A jolt of air hit my throat and I began to gag. Michael gripped my lower jaw to stop me from biting my tongue.

"Mr. Choy," he said. "Like this." He took in a deep breath, then slowly, loudly, exhaled. I pulled in the deepest breath I could and followed suit. Slowly. Loudly. A monitor began to beep in steady rhythm with the rise and fall of my lungs.

As a thin tube pumped moist oxygen through my nose, I gulped to taste the air on my tongue. I swallowed. *I could breathe on my own.* The ventilator was gone.

After a few minutes, I began to play: breathing deeper, then slower, swallowing quickly, gulping faster, while the tapping beeps sang out and danced along with the alternating pressure in my lungs, Ginger Rogers to my Fred Astaire.

Michael laughed. "Are we showing off?"

Delighted, I relaxed and let myself breathe with a natural, steady rhythm. I heard no angels singing.

~~~

The medical team had decided to switch medications and gradually to wean me off the sedatives. I became more alert, but I still had to struggle with my vocal abilities.

A woman with a soft voice politely asked me if I wanted my hair washed. "You'll feel so much better, Mr. Choy," she continued.

"Here?" I asked, barely able to push out the first sound.

"Let me wash it for you."

The nurse lifted my head as her assistant slipped a rubberized mat snugly under my neck. A Niagara of warm water poured down. Sturdy fingers worked shampoo into my oily, sweat-matted mop and massaged my tingling scalp. A last rinse rained down.

"Finished."

Thick towels soaked up the pool of water, while a rough towel blotted my wet head, and then the rubber mat was pulled away. The two women began to discuss their shift changes for the coming week. A comb pulled across my damp hair. The topic switched to a sale at the Eaton Centre. I took a deep breath. I tasted apple shampoo.

"Beautiful silver-grey hair, Mr. Choy," the woman said. "Almost as thick as my own."

"Please call me Wayson," I said, surprised to hear myself speaking so clearly. If they'd call me Wayson, then I'd be set free. I could push myself up and walk out of the hospital. Mr. Choy was the sick one, not Wayson.

"Please, *please* call me Wayson."

"Well, Wayson," came the friendly response, "you're sure you don't want us to call you a taxi?"

⌒

Jumbles of sounds and images drifted in and out of what seemed my waking moments. Sensations of touch, taste, and smell randomly came to me, vivid three-dimensional fragments trapped between sleep and wakefulness. I was Alice, tumbling ever deeper down the rabbit hole of some parallel existence. Struggling to be heard beyond a whisper, I dropped the *please* and *thank you*, grew short-tempered.

Gary's hand brushed my forehead, but the gesture did not bring me any relief.

"E.T. go home," I managed. "Why can't I go home?"

"You're not strong enough, Wayson."

"You're not the doctor," I snapped.

"Jean wants to give you a kiss," Gary said. And Jean bent down and kissed me.

"Where's Tosh?"

"She's gone back to Arizona," Jean said. "She just couldn't stay any longer, Wayson."

In a moment of clarity, seeing Jean's eyes tearing up, I understood. When Tosh had heard I was in intensive care, she phoned St. Michael's from Arizona, contrived to query the head nurse about my condition, and immediately flew to Toronto. That evening when the medical team could not calm me down during my "cardiac event," Tosh, my late-night visitor, had waved her hand to offer her help.

"I'm a cardiac nurse," she told them. Her eyes must have flashed with some authority.

"Are you on staff here?"

"No. But this man has been my godfather since I was four."

One of the doctors looked at the others. "Step up here," he said. "He won't listen to us. Can you talk to him?"

She did.

I listened, and calmed down.

What a circle of life that moment represented to me. When Tosh was thirteen I had tried some child psychology to calm her down after her shouting match with her mother. I long ago forgot what the problem might have been between them, but I remember thinking it was something I could easily solve between a fit-to-be-tied mother and a screaming daughter—a bachelor's folly to think so. I knocked on her bedroom door. Eyes red with crying, she opened it for me. Her child's radar was on.

"You should listen to your mother," I began, and launched into the importance of being patient with someone as caring as Jean.

She caught my lecturing tone. And as she listened to that hoary idea about her now becoming a young, mature woman, she saw through my condescending way.

"You don't know what you're talking about," she said, her eyes narrowing, fists clenched. Then she hollered for the whole house to hear, "*None of you know anything!*"

And slammed the door in my face.

Jean looked up from the bottom of the stairs. "You, too, Wayson?"

"What do you mean?"

"Oh, nothing," she said. "Tosh just welcomed you as an equal member of the family."

"Oh," I said, mentally rubbing my bruised ego. "That's good to know."

"I'll talk to her later." She offered me a cigarette. We both lit up.

"Just think, Wayson, one day we'll be old and decrepit and have to listen to *her.* Let's hope she does a better job."

"Karma," I said.

I'm here, Wayson, Tosh had said. *Calm down.*

That was all she'd had to say. *I'm here.* I had settled down. Straps were tightened, then loosened, and I slept.

Awake, I could tell it was late into the night. No one was around. The halls of the recovery ward, where I had been for forty-eight hours, were silent. I called out for water, mouthing with a clenched throat, *Thirs-teee . . . wa- wa-tor, please . . .*

Out of the gloom, a bald orderly sauntered by holding a beaker of water. When I lifted my hand to reach for it, he disappeared. But a clear plastic cup temptingly brimming with water shimmered beside my pillow. I reached out again. My arm fell back, too weak to lift itself.

"No," someone snapped. "Don't touch that."

A stern little woman in green scrubs darted towards me and positioned herself at my bedside table. She stood just tall enough to stare into my face through her wire-rimmed glasses. Her tone was harsh: "You're not getting any, Mr. Choy."

"But I'm thirsty."

"You're not to have any water." The woman's broad face and red brow registered blunt indifference. When she spoke, her crooked teeth dripped with spidery lines of saliva. "All the water in this hospital belongs to me."

She snatched the shining tumbler off the metal table and held it a few inches beyond my grasp. The water wavered, reflecting the overhead lamps. A few drops fell onto her scrubs.

"I'm the Queen of Water," she announced. "In this ward, no one gets any water without my permission. Do you have a requisition for this?"

She stepped back, smiled triumphantly, and fingered the rim of the plastic cup as if she held a crystal chalice. I tried to shout: desperate, raspy sounds escaped into the air. She turned her back on me and stomped away, jolting the tumbler in her grasp so that water spilled everywhere.

The Queen of Water appeared three times at my bedside,

looking down at me with her bullet eyes. Each time I tried to stop her from stealing my glass, but I couldn't move. Her thick-soled feet scampered up a small flight of stairs to a landing floating just ten feet above me. She swung open a cupboard door. Rows and rows of shelves glistened with clear cups of water.

I complained to one of the nurses who bent down beside me, her ear close to my mouth. She took notes.

"Queen of Water," I said. "Stop her."

"I'm going to report her to the doctor," the nurse said. "Don't you worry, Mr. Choy."

"Tell the doctors," I blurted out. "Tell Tosh."

Exhausted, I shut my eyes.

"Give him 20 more milligrams," a voice said.

Even though at times barely awake, through my lashes I glimpsed them all—my designated powers of attorney, Karl and Marie, Gary and Jean—all my family standing around my bed, whispering. Even when they stood silently over my skeletal frame, I could see how they sustained each other with clasped hands and nodding heads. I had given each of them a terrible authority: to let me die if the medical situation was hopeless. Apparently, a half dozen times when I was most out of it, my situation looked hopeless.

But whenever I saw them through the haze, I wanted to tell them, *I feel better—please, please stop fretting.*

"No, no," I began. "All . . . all . . . fine . . ."

I wanted to tell them how I almost sat up by myself, without pillows; that the dizzy spell lasted only a few seconds; and that when my head bumped against the raised edge of the bed, I felt nothing at all.

Nothing.

And that I had the wit to pull the cord at the last instant before that bump knocked me out.

And that the nurse they called Michael told me how the charts all showed I was making steady improvement, and that the medical team declared it a good sign that I tried to sit up on my own, had collapsed, and tried again, sputtered, spat, and laughed. The laughter was the sign they took to be my saving grace.

"He was laughing at himself," one of the nurses reported. "The doctors think he's on his way to recovery now."

No one argued. I was officially recovering. No one knew that I had somehow taken a psychologically dark turn: inside, I was losing hope.

I had struggled to ask for a pen and paper, and one of the nurses on the night shift had made out my words. He brought me both and guided my fingers to them. Pen and paper slipped away from me. Two, three, four times. The family was told about this. When I felt myself fully awake, I could not reach for the cups of water left behind for me. When I woke up, every cup had disappeared. I knew who had snatched them away. None of the family seemed able to make out my confusing explanations. Finally, they must have been given the nurse's notes.

"The Queen of Water can't get into this ward, Wayson." It was Mary Jo explaining things to me. "The hospital has posted a guard at the entrance to stop her."

"Karl and Gary are right here standing guard, too," Marie said.

"We're all keeping our eyes out for her," Jean said. "There's no way she can get back in here."

Everyone nodded. I nodded back. And then they, too, were gone.

⁓

Again I called for water. Unable to fetch it myself, unable to have things instantly my own way, I wanted revenge on every immovable limb, on everything that wouldn't go my way. Enraged, I wanted to end my maddening thirst.

"Water," I groaned.

A smiling head stood over me.

"Open wide, Mr. Choy." The man's broad smile was reassuring. "You can't use a cup yet. I'm sorry. How about a spongy swab with moisture for your throat?" He grinned, as if urging me to reconstruct some pleasant dream: it was the nurse they called Michael. *Michelangelo.* I vaguely knew him. He examined my opened mouth. "Yes, some swabs will help." As he stepped behind the grey curtains, he said, "You've had this treat a few times already, but I guess you don't remember."

I did remember.

Those moist swabs Michael had gently pressed against the parched membranes of my mouth to release a droplet or two of flavoured liquid. With my throat on fire all those days on the ventilator, I had craved the simplest of all relief—relief not only from the fear of dying from thirst, but from the fear of not feeling again the simple acts that can connect one human being to another.

"Open up," Michael said, with dutiful innocence. "Try this one—it's grape-flavoured."

He gently tapped my cheek. I opened up. Another swab touched my tongue. In an instant a taste like the best Shiraz. I crushed my tongue against the spongy end. Like the monk of Zen legend reaching for a grape as he hung on to a cliff-edged vine, the second the branch snapped, I gulped, unabashedly smacking my lips.

Michael laughed.

⟶

Michael was real. He came back every hour or two and waved another prescribed swab in front of me.

Michael was a keeper, as Marie would often say of Karl, meaning he was one of those rare men whose inner qualities outshone their good looks.

"Open up, Mr. Choy."

"*Wayson*," I said. "Call me Wayson."

The swab touched my lips; it too was real, and the plush tip was saturated with liquid. My tongue squeezed against the soaked blob. An instant crush of chilled lemony fluid dripped into the back of my mouth and pooled. I swallowed. With the second and third swabs, I held my tongue against the cottony ends and trapped the lingering moisture on my palate. A primal pleasure gripped me: lips smacked, greedy for more refreshment.

"Nice to see you so happy, Wayson," Michael said. "I think you might like some icy bits. Remember them?"

I did remember: finely crushed ice spooned onto my tongue. If I found the humble swabs to be my first salvation, reviving my interest in tasting all life had to offer again, the icy bits were sensationally even better.

A hand—had it been Michael's or Tosh's?—would wipe the drool from the corner of my mouth. Like a desert beggar, I would bend my head back and yawn with all my strength to welcome the cascading chips of ice. Now I wanted to feel that cold again, drenching much more than my thirst. For a spoonful of icy bits, I would battle the growing darkness around me, that sense of helplessness creeping over me: *Would I ever write again? Didn't I have a book to finish? Would these thin-veined fingers manage to tap away on a keyboard—or even hold a pen to paper?*

"Here—open wide."

As the tiny shards spilled onto my tongue, crackling cold against my teeth, whisperings and images uncoiled in my head: *We thought we lost you . . . nearly died on us . . .* wan faces with open collars fretted and complained about the humidity outside; someone sang a lullaby; someone else unfolded crinkling pages and read aloud from a book. Fingers brushed my cheek. Lips pressed my forehead.

This was the moment, the instant when even the sickest cell in my body, my most despondent self, rallied for an extra second of life.

"You're doing so much better, Mr. Choy." It was the doctor pulling aside the curtain. "I have a pill for you tonight. Michael says you're swallowing now without too much coughing or choking. You'll be ready to try some solid food soon. Let's see how you get this pill down."

Michael gave me a cup of water and stepped aside.

I swallowed.

Coughed only once.

⌒

With great hope, my family now visited to witness my performance as the Recovering Corpse.

They saw me propped up against a pile of pillows and applauded my upright position. Marie reminded me that I had actually eaten some pudding that morning. I couldn't remember taking in any food by mouth, but Jean said, "The nurse told me you even asked for a second helping."

I licked my teeth and tasted vanilla.

Chapter 5

I OPENED MY EYES AND FOUND MYSELF IN ANOTHER
room, dimly lit. My younger goddaughter, Kate, sitting in a chair
beside me, had just finished high school and was getting ready
to leave home for the first time to enter university in Montreal.
But once, she had climbed up the stairs to my room on her
sturdy five-year-old legs and interrupted me at my desk with a
drawing fresh from her kingdom of crayons and papers.
"Daddy's day," she informed me, and handed over her latest
work: three stick figures standing together, her mother, father,
and, drawn half-sized, herself. To the side stood another stick
figure, with a large head and a scruffy chin. Above this bearded
balloon head she had carefully printed in capital letters WAYSON,
and at a slant, DADDY 2. She gave me a hug and ran away.

Propped against my pillows, too tired now to focus on what
Kate was asking me in her grown-up voice, I barely nodded
my head.

She repeated the question for the third time.

"Do—you—*need*—*any*—thing?"

I attempted once more to answer, but managed only to slur my words and gasp for breath. I tried again. Kate pretended not to be disturbed. I tried to raise my head. Impossible. It weighed a ton. Kate told me she saw my fingers drumming in frustration.

"Wayson," she said. "Spell out what you want. I'm going to say the alphabet and you tap your finger on my hand when I get to the letter you mean. Nod your head."

I nodded.

"A . . . B . . ."

I tapped twice.

"B?" she asked.

I tapped again to signal yes.

And so it went. I wasn't always attentive. Some letters I didn't catch, and when my fingers drummed in confusion, she began at A again.

"Is this what you want: 'Bring me some of my clothes'?" Kate said.

I nodded.

After she left me, Kate complained to Mary Jo, "Just like an English teacher! All he had to do was spell out *two* words, 'bring clothes,' or just *one* word, 'clothes.' But *he* had to spell out a *complete* six-word sentence!"

⌒

"You look like you've lost a bit of weight, Mr. Choy." It was the orderly.

I remembered again where I was: *Still* alive, I thought.

"Get more rest now, sir," he said, tucking in a corner of the sheet. "You've had so many visitors. Everybody tells us they're your family.

"There've been dozens and dozens of people in the waiting room," he went on. "They keep coming and coming, and they all want to visit you. They all swear they're family. The head nurse had to set limits." His deep laugh shook my ears.

"All those white faces, those redheads and blonds, and all of them insisting that they're your family—did you know about that? And the nurse told me only two of them were Asian."

I tried to guess who the two Asians could be: Was it Kerri, who is Japanese? Jean, the Korean? Judy? Or was it a Richard— the Chinese or the Caribbean-Chinese one? Did any of them even know I was in the hospital?

And who were those "dozens and dozens" of non-Asians who had called themselves family?

I recalled white faces with Celtic and Anglo-Saxon names; then, spontaneously, more foreign-sounding names matched to their Jewish, Greek, Italian, and East European features floated by. Behind each face the sky was blue and the sun shone. *How odd*, I thought, observing the parade, *they all look Asian to me.*

⌐

Voices filtered through my memory during that second and third week of recovery.

Denise, my durable literary agent, was reading to me, loudly intoning dramatic phrases and paragraphs, even through some erotic passages. Someone tried to shush her up.

"He's able to hear," said Denise to whomever was demanding some quiet, "and I'm *making sure* he hears. Keeps his brain active."

Kate took over the reading from Denise. Kate's voice shook nervously, then grew softer. Her rhythm, like a lullaby, lulled me into a long sleep, so that I woke up refreshed for the first time.

"Hello?" a voice said. "Is anyone there?"

It was my voice. I could see beyond the bed rail: the door was open and someone came towards me.

"Well, Mr. Choy," said a tall man. He introduced himself as my new supervising doctor. He made a show of looking over my charts. "You're getting better every day. I figure we'll be moving you to another spot very soon. Get some more rest."

Marie stepped into the room, dressed for work in a beautiful summer print.

"Just to sit with you before I meet my next client," she said, as if she could spare the time.

An image came to me of her bending over my father's bare feet, clipping his toenails. I had had trouble dressing him that morning. His socks would catch on his overgrown nails, sharp and yellow. I was looking in the phone book for someone who did pedicures.

"I can do that," Marie said.

"No, no," Father protested, embarrassed at his own son's reluctance to do the tricky task.

"No trouble at all," Marie said. "I used to volunteer at the seniors' home. Don't you trust me, Toy?"

Father beamed. He was in love.

As she stepped into the sunlight of my hospital room, tall and elegant, I imagined how my father must have seen her.

"Marie," I said, "you look beautiful."

"Stop," she said. "You'll never be as good a flirt as your father was."

⌒

"It's me, Wayson," Karl said, nudging me alert.

I nodded, *Yes.*

He reminded me that I had been admitted into the hospital on the ninth of August. It was now the last week of August. Toronto was still in the grip of a terrible heat wave. People fainted in the streets. He told me that seniors stuck in suffocating rooms were told to spend their afternoons in air-conditioned malls.

"Or they can join me," I said. "I think I've memorized every crack in this ceiling."

"Would you like to sit up?"

Without pausing for an answer, he sat on the bed and pulled me up against his side like a rag doll. He doubled up the two pillows to support my back. I leaned into him. His work shirt smelled of wood shavings.

Still fighting drug withdrawal, I felt a little dizzy. I couldn't see clearly beyond the few feet lit by some kind of lamp, yet Karl looked at me as if witnessing some miracle. I was up. Talking. He put his arm around me.

A few months ago, he had lost his father, a handsome, muscular man of seventy-four who had been a teenaged German soldier when the war ended. Just before his surrender, he had a chance to shoot an American soldier attempting to take a shit in the distant bushes, his unbuttoned trousers clearly down around his ankles.

"Who should die that way?" Karl's father had asked himself. He told his son, "Man is not an animal." The young soldier lowered his weapon, and in that second an Allied soldier tackled him from behind, disarmed him, and took him prisoner. If he had pulled that trigger, he would have been shot himself. That single bullet would have ended any chance that I would now be chatting about the weather and leaning against him, that Marie or Kate would have ever come into my life. How our lives are now woven together the direct result of someone needing to take a crap and a boy-soldier who would not shoot him.

Karl and his father often sat together in their farmhouse kitchen up north and talked long into the night like old friends, of justice and philosophy, and the corrupting power of the corporate rich.

I envied the depth of their debates, their mutual respect and attachment. My own father was a distant figure until the end of his life. My father's English was far more useful than my child's vocabulary of Toishanese words, but his was a survivor's English, a practical tool for the kitchens and restaurant counters where he earned his living.

Our fathers told stories about the past, but rarely dwelled upon the terrors of famine or war. Neither did they say much about the painful humiliations they had suffered as undesirable immigrants to Canada.

"Old times," my father would say, "bad times."

In our twenty-five years under the same roof, Karl and I had had only two or three shouting matches. "Like watching Titans duelling," Marie once said after one of our self-righteous battles in which nothing was harmed but my ego. "Now, kiss and make up," she would say, and the ripples of our disagreement subsided.

The day Karl sat on the bed and held me so I could lean back against his arm, I saw the exhaustion in his eyes. I wanted to tell him that one of the doctors had told me how, with the mix of drugs that had been prescribed for me, I might later experience some difficulties with my metabolism and blood counts.

"You're not out of the woods yet," the doctor had said. "But you'll be ready to get up and walk around in them."

I said nothing to Karl. It came to me, in some unspoken way, that I had to find my own way through those woods. Besides, I liked resting silently in his arms.

TWO

The youth gets together his materials to build a bridge to the moon, or, perchance, a palace or temple on the earth, and, at length, the middle-aged man concludes to build a woodshed with them.

–Henry David Thoreau, Journal

Chapter 6

⁓

TWO ORDERLIES CAME ONE EVENING AND WOKE ME FROM a deep sleep. "Sliding under you, Mr. Choy . . . easy does it." They gently folded the bedsheets, lifted, and laid me down on a thin mattress on top of a stretcher. After being wheeled through a series of hallways and into a deep elevator, we waited in a brightly lit reception area before a pair of imposing plate-glass doors.

"Mr. Choy?" The same baritone voice penetrated the dull roar in my head. "In a minute, someone will let us in." Then a whisper crept into my ear, as if we were in a sanctuary: *Private room, Mr. Choy. Very best for you.*

I whispered back, *I want to go home.* But no one moved. *Take me home.*

I focused my eyes to peer through to the other side of the glass doors and couldn't help but notice a stretcher bearing an elderly patient waiting for these same doors to unlock. *Traffic jam,* I thought. Still a little groggy, I gave the poor guy what I hoped was an encouraging smile.

He raised his taut brow to look back at me. His sunken cheeks gave his chiselled head the look of a skull attempting to smile back. In the night quiet between us, he looked distant and terrible. I shifted my head and saw the man's darkly bruised and withered neck tilt upwards. The skull grinned and stared back at me. The eyes widened, as if stunned. Those eyes, ringed with exhaustion, looked familiar. The creature squinting back at me seemed barely alive. Those eyes shut down in disbelief were my own. My spirit plummeted.

A tall shadow erased my shocked reflection. "Press in the code," the shadow commanded. Fingers rapidly tapped at a panel of buttons, and with a buzzing sound, both wide doors swung open to reveal a spacious lounge, empty except for a solitary nurse who stood waiting for us.

I was wheeled into the first room to the left, lifted up and onto a bed. The bed rails were raised and loudly snapped into place. I was in an adult crib. "For your safety, Mr. Choy," the voice explained. The nurse signed some forms—I imagined she checked off "Body Received As Is"—and waved the two men away.

"Mr. Choy?" I heard her say. "I need you to swallow this tiny pill. Please open up. It's to help you go back to sleep. Can you see that I'm holding the cup and straw by your mouth?"

As is, I thought. My lips touched the straw, and I took a couple of sips and swallowed the tiny pill.

The overhead lights were turned off. The room was dark, except for a dim nightlight near the floor and the frame of soft light coming from the hall. I should have fallen asleep within minutes, but adrenalin kept me alert. When the nurse had offered me water I had noticed, as if for the first time, that I hadn't been able to reach for the cup, nor was I able to direct the straw to my mouth.

It occurred to me then that I couldn't quite raise my arms. I couldn't grasp simple objects like spoons or cups for more than a few seconds. For days I had agreed with anyone who was sympathetic that I was still too weak, still too early in my recovery. I would nod my head or shrug my shoulders in response, unable to sum up the energy to complete a full sentence without coughing or gagging.

A shimmer of dim light on the far wall gave me the sense that I was launching into stormy seas. My mind tossed through my semi-comatose stages in the ICU. Through half-opened lids I saw how some friends had shaken in horror at my strapped wrists, how others reached out to hold my sweat-damp palms. And then there were those who turned and quickly left, weeping.

Now I felt the dread that had marked their faces. *Will I ever teach or write again? Walk again? Will I be the same person I was?*

I tried to blame the tiny pill I had just swallowed for the panic that swelled inside me. I wondered if the feeling was a symptom of some chemical withdrawal. It swallowed me again. I might lie helpless in this bed for my remaining days. I might die.

I stared at the pool of light streaming in from the hall. I could crawl over the gates of this bed and sink deeply into those waves, fall into my narcotic sleep and never wake up.

I heard my own child's voice call out to me, a voice whose tongue was rooted in the stubborn, insatiable curiosity that was still squirming inside me; a voice that nagged the elders for more stories, whether from an ancient fable or a folk tale. That child would defy any bedtime rules and willingly give away his share of sleep: "Tell me," I would beg my storytelling elders, "tell me, what happens next?"

I heard a loud knock, and a slight middle-aged woman stepped into the gloom and apologized for troubling me.

"I'm recently arrived from Dublin," she said. "Still getting used to this night shift. Hope you don't mind, but I'm a bit behind in the schedule." She snapped on the bedside lamp. Her glasses danced with the light as she noted my name stuck on the bedpost. "Hope you weren't sleeping, Mr. Choy."

She reached down one side of the bed and pushed a button. The bed sank lower. She explained what she was there to do, then pulled back the sheets. Without any prudish concerns, she expertly adjusted my nighttime catheter and slipped a long pair of medical tights over my legs.

"To prevent blood clots from forming in your legs, Mr. Choy," she explained. "A pair of nun's stockings, sure it is!" She reminded me that St. Michael's was once run by an order of nuns. "The best nuns still wear them! And if you don't mind me saying so, I think in Dublin some of the best priests do, too!" She shook her head. "Just look at those bony legs! Don't you crave good food, Mr. Choy?" she said before pulling the sheets back over me.

Finished with washing her hands at the sink, she held up a small, unopened juice bottle. "What's this?" she said, her smile comforting. She twisted the cap off, slipped in a straw she pulled out of thin air. "A bit of grape someone left for you."

She firmly palmed the back of my head and lifted. The thin straw slipped into my mouth. Without thinking, I reached up with my right hand; my fingers took hold of the bottle; the small hand withdrew. I sipped and swallowed, thirsting for more sweetness. Against the gush of grape juice, the tip of my tongue began to lick the back of my molars for delicious bits of remembered feasts. With the salt taste of roasts and steaks, and of tender boneless chicken smothered in Chinese black bean sauce, with the turnaround logic of something like hope, I took a giant gulp, and loudly slurped up the last drops.

"Well, Mr. Choy," she said, "I bet you eat as loudly as you drink. All Chinese people do!"

She must have guessed that I would not mind: she made the sign of the cross over me and gently touched my shoulder. Her glasses reflected back the tears brimming in my eyes.

"You hurry and get better now," she said, and snapped off the lamp. "Promise?"

I promised myself I would eat, and eat even more.

The next morning, pondering the disturbances of the night before, which I recalled only vaguely now, I concluded that I had simply had a bad dream or an upset stomach caused by that tiny pill. "You lucky boy," Mother used to say to me when I was a child and woke up crying. "You only dream bad luck." Daylight leaked in the edges of a heavily draped window to my left. A nurse came in and raised the top half of the bed at an angle high enough that if I turned my head I could see outside. She put her hands on the heavy drapes.

"Get ready for the sunlight, Mr. Choy," she said. "Shade your eyes."

She threw the drapes open and light flooded the room. The room was on the sixth floor, I was told, looking down on one of Toronto's classic churches across the street. Spiral towers thrust like arrows into the air. Bells and chimes rang out. Using only my fists, I managed to push myself higher up on the bed and lifted my head until I could see the summer grass below. The beige brick-and-stone walls, the decorated shell-shaped entrances and exits glowed like a caramel-coloured wedding cake. Then I fell back down into the pillow, still feeling a little drugged. On my right side, the ceiling curve of curtains had been drawn around my bed to offer privacy from the open doorway.

Lying in the morning sunlight, I remembered I had vowed to someone during the night that I would eat, and eat more. I stretched out my legs, surprised that they moved so readily on my command. I lifted the sheets with cooperative fingers and looked down. I could make out the tops of finely knitted tights drawn up like those hip-waders worn by fishermen casting in deep waters.

A clanging of dishes came into the room. A breakfast of porridge and mashed fruit had arrived, with an assistant to spoon it into me.

I settled nicely into that too comfortable bed. Slowly turning to my side, reaching down with a shaky hand, using levers to raise and lower the top half of it, I was determined to sit up and greet my visitors. I no longer required a catheter. The attending nurse showed me how to tug at the call bell when I needed the bedpan.

My second morning, I was helped out of bed to see how well I could stand up by myself. My hands instinctively gripped the bed rails, and I hauled myself straight up. The nurse pulled back the privacy curtain. The room was fitted for another bed, but the space was empty.

"You might be able to use the bathroom in your room now. Want to try?"

I grunted back a few words and nodded, *Yes, yes.* Leaning on her, I managed to make it to the toilet, sit down, finished my business, and pulled the cord for her assistance back to my bed. Hobble-stepping between the facilities and the curtained-off bed, I could see a parade of strangers and patients greet each other as they walked past in the hall. Wheelchairs and crutches went by; canes tapped on the floor; chattering and laughter rose and fell. I was asked if I might like to sit in a wheelchair myself and leave the room. I refused. I wanted to join the parade only on foot, even if held up by one of the contraptions supporting so many of those patients stumbling past me now. I wanted to walk again. One time when I had to get out of bed and struggle to the toilet on the arm of a nurse or orderly, the bed rail on one side was lowered, and I grunted and gestured for it to stay down so that I could practise getting off the bed.

My first few attempts to stand by myself were crushed by the effort just to hold my head up. The attempt to take a few independent steps saw me trip and stumble up against my guardian. However, with each subsequent try, my limbs and neck muscles did gain in strength. And the best of those limb-struggling days return to me now like a single, unbroken Hollywood narrative, complete with the triumphant theme from *Rocky.*

The march to victory began one morning after breakfast when the enthusiastic physiotherapist—"Call me Allison"—with her golden braids and blue eyes, observed my assisted foot-slog to the bathroom and decided I could "seriously start walking." With a big smile, Allison strapped a pair of weights to my ankles. I raised and lowered and turned both feet at her command. I barely started getting used to them when Allison tugged at her braided hair and announced, "You're ready for a walker, Mr. Choy," and came back with a metal walker and demonstrated how to use it.

I pushed forward on the walker and took a first step. Allison let me lean on her for the second step. Then another.

"Use your hips and move your shoulders—like this," she said, and demonstrated.

I stumbled, fell against her, straightened myself up. Tried again.

"Use your hips to push forward," she said. "Don't use your arms or the walker to pull you along."

I threw the weight of my hip forward. My foot followed. Allison was delighted.

"Now we're dancing. Keep moving, Mr. Choy."

I repeated the hip-step pattern and made it across the room and back, five times, and then into my bathroom. I excused myself, pushed the door shut, and took the opportunity to sit like a conquering hero on the throne. I walked the length of the room twice more. Close to dropping to the floor and gasping with exhaustion, I nearly gave up. From across the room, Allison flung my puffer at me. Without thinking, I snatched it from the air with one hand. Surprised, Allison applauded. *Victory.*

I was not out of the woods yet, but I sensed I had survived the worst, and surviving felt good. I became a kind of student again, answering questions, completing tests, taking instructions.

I didn't entirely pass taking instructions with flying colours. Once, when one nurse refused to stay a moment to listen carefully to my grunting request for a fresh glass of water, I retaliated by spitting out the pill she had asked me to swallow.

"It's for your own good," she said, and put down the tray and left me to shift for myself, the tiny pill spinning on the tray placed just beyond my reach.

Whenever I would complain to my father about promising students whom I seemed unable to reach, who instead would spit back my lessons, he would sit back and say, "When the student is ready, the right teacher will arrive."

In the universe of my half-empty hospital room, the right teachers began to arrive. I became more patient with those who cared for me, acted like the student I wished others had been for me.

One woman came at breakfast and positioned my fingers correctly around each utensil. By her second visit, I had relearned how to hold a spoon, to hold a fork, tines down, and to slide a dull knife with ease across a slab of greyish meatloaf; I even managed to feed myself the entire inedible dinner with no serious mishaps, though not without a wide bib tucked beneath my chin.

A therapist came to test my fine motor skills. I was instructed to cut up a blank sheet of paper to see how I managed with a pair of scissors. At first, my fingers fumbled in an all-thumbs fashion, though I could see in my mind the proper way to manipulate them. She positioned my fingers, then let me try the scissors again. On the third attempt the piece of white paper on which I had crayoned strokes of reds and yellows curled away from the blades like a pair of fiery wings.

Delighted with my success, and grateful to her, I took one of the uncut sheets of paper and attempted to fold for her an origami butterfly—a specialty of mine—to demonstrate my dexterity. The therapist waited until I was finished.

Finally, I gave up and handed over the mess.

"How nice," she cheerfully said. "An envelope."

After my personal-history questions were completed, I was asked by another therapist to concentrate on cartoon pictures of a hat, a doll, a dog, a spoon. I did okay when recalling the objects but was unable to hold any numbers in my head. It had always been my good fortune to be bad with figures. I failed accounting tests in high school and so failed to enter a Chinatown-approved profession; instead, I took my majors in subjects that interested me—sociology, English literature, and creative writing.

The women around the clicking mah-jong tables warned Mother about my academic choices.

"Why won't your son study for business or science?"

"What salary will Wayson make with just studying fancy books? And what about his stories? Who buy them?"

"Sonny needs to make lots of money to have a good family and good children and a good house," an elder told Mother.

"Get him marry soon. Who take care of him when he is old and you not there any more?"

"What good his degree? Useless, I guarantee!"

"That's what they're saying about you," my Aunt Freda told me. "You want my opinion? Do what you damn well like. I wish I had that chance."

"Professor de Bruyn told me your story got into *Prism* magazine!" Aunt Mary exclaimed at my graduation from UBC. "That's a good sign."

At the ceremony, my father stood proud, but my mother looked out of place, and worried. Many of the graduating sons and daughters of Old Chinatown were being recruited for jobs in banks, businesses, hospitals, clinics, international corporations, and, best of all, government offices. And what about the Choys' son? That aimless, book-loving boy was talking some foolishness about hitchhiking to Ottawa to fight racial discrimination. *What salary for such a son?*

My mother would sit quietly listening to all the unasked-for advice. She then would come home, find me reading a book or typing away on another story, and make me some tea. My father had instructed her not to interfere with my studies.

To read and write—that was what the scholars of Old China valued. My grandfather, who had been educated at a level that the community in Victoria's Chinatown had respected, had raised Father. Unlike Grandfather, Father ended his own studies when he came to Gold Mountain as a teenager. In Victoria, Father was the First Son and had to work beside Grandfather, earning his keep for the old man's and his stepmother's growing Victoria family, which soon numbered six boys and four girls. When he married my mother, the two left for Vancouver to make their own life together. By then, any schooling was out of the question, but Father never forgot the respect given to the scholars and educated merchants of Chinatown. When he came home from his seasonal work as a chef on the CPR steamship lines, he took pleasure in my shelves of books— volumes that neither he nor Mother could read. When I typed away at my stories, he asked about my grades in English literature.

"Got another A," I said.

I graduated from UBC and my first published story was anthologized in *Best American Short Stories,* a story of a boy who challenges his older friend to swim in the Moira River— *Caucasian* boys, they were—Father bought me the Parker fountain pen with a 14-karat gold nib from Birks that I had always meant one day to buy for myself.

"You write with this," he said. "Tell people the stories that you remember from your grandfather and all those elders who took care of you."

We shared a rare hug. But even as I held him, I frowned at his naiveté, his utter foolishness: where were there readers and movie producers for stories about the elders of Chinatown or, for that matter, about anyone from Chinatown? In my narratives, the characters were given European surnames and greeted their world with pale faces.

"How is he going to earn a good salary?" Mother asked aloud at my graduation.

"He'll find his own way," Father said, with a wink at me. "How else?"

Looking at the crescent moon from my hospital bed and thinking of all this, I imagined among the stars my father winking at me. I longed to wink back, to hold once again that fountain pen, which I somehow lost hitchhiking to Ottawa.

Chapter 7

ONE AFTERNOON, MARIE WAS READING ME THE LATEST bunch of funny get-well cards and missing-you notes. My voice was still croaky, but I could be understood.

"What's the matter, Wayson?" Marie asked.

"I want to be cremated."

"Yes, you said exactly that when I first walked you into emergency. Karl thought it was very cheerful of you."

"I want to be a good-looking corpse at my funeral but not just yet," I said. "Once I have gained a little weight and don't look so bad . . ." I coughed. "What am I doing stuck in a locked-in ward?"

I noted Marie's too-broad smile.

"You're just here for a few more days, that's all." Her sigh, a little too exaggerated. "There's no other place to put you. Something about budget cuts."

Gary and Jean came in just then, and catching the clue thrown by Marie, Jean immediately picked up the conversational ball.

"That's right, Wayson," she said. "And you're so much better in a private room like this."

Jean smiled, Gary smiled, and Marie hung on to her smile. Jean changed the subject.

"The nurse gave this to me. Remember? You asked for seconds on the pudding."

"That's a good sign," said Gary. He snapped off the plastic spoon taped to the side of the Styrofoam cup. I let him slip a fresh bib under my chin. A supply had been put on the shelf above my bed.

"I hate pudding," I said. "I'm only eating to get back to the Pearl Court for a banquet dinner."

Lifting the first spoonful to my mouth, Gary said, "Everything's going to be fine. Here."

Fine, I thought, and found myself wanting to tell the family that something had made me unhappy when I was first wheeled into this new wing.

"How do you like those doors?" I asked.

I wanted to tell them that something—something connected to those plate-glass doors—was troubling me, but nothing specific came to mind. An awkward silence descended over everyone.

Gary finally said, "Oh, they weren't any problem for us."

"You look great in this bed," Jean said. "All those big pillows look so comfortable. Don't you feel good, Wayson?"

I felt well enough to make a few demands. Give some orders.

"Marie," I said, "can you please remember to bring me one of those blank notebooks from my upstairs bookshelf?" I turned to Gary. "I have my favourite fountain pen in my desk at school. Can you please remember to bring it next time?" I got back my announcement-in-class voice. I took for granted

I had never lost it. "I've decided while I'm in here recovering, I'll be writing some new chapters."

Marie and Jean looked at each other.

"What's wrong?" I asked.

"Nothing," Marie said. "It's just the way you're talking."

"I always talk like this," I said, and wondered why everyone seemed so surprised.

Jean smiled encouragingly. "You're actually going to write in here?" Gary gave me a thumbs-up.

It hadn't completely dawned on me that if I was having trouble just *thinking* of using the spoon, it would be next to impossible to use a pen. My desire to write was so overwhelming that my mind dismissed my obvious shortcomings. My post-coma brain failed to acknowledge any such disparities: one half of the grey cells craving normalcy didn't always connect with what the other half was still incapable of doing.

The pudding finished, Gary threw the cup and spoon into the garbage can under the sink.

"Don't forget to bring me that pen," I said. "I want to use the Mont Blanc that Earl gave me for Christmas—you remember?—the year before he died. I think René, Tony, and Evelyn all chipped in, too. If you can't find it in my desk, ask Kit to look in the back of my filing drawer at Humber. Tell her to look for that leather pouch I keep the pen in . . ."

I continued rattling on about the pen and described the particular notebook I wanted from the house. They all just nodded. Perhaps I was being too demanding. Nagging. That happens among family members.

"I'm glad you remember Earl," Gary finally said.

"Of course," I said. "I'll never forget Earl."

They each gave me a kiss on the cheek, excusing themselves to meet other appointments. In the sudden quiet of my room, I could hear them moving away from my door. Someone joined them, and I heard Gary almost shouting down the hall:

"Doctor, he's talking in full sentences!"

Despite the days that I spent in the lock-down unit, the Mont Blanc never arrived. Nor did Marie deliver any blank notebooks. I couldn't quite appreciate then that my time in St. Michael's was burning out those family members and friends closest to me. In fact, by the evening of that same day, after some more pills, I had forgotten that I had even asked for pen or paper. And if Karl visited me with Kate, who was back from Montreal, as he confirmed to me on the phone that same night, I could not remember.

My two families had exhausted their time and energy with me. I was still suffering the effects of withdrawal from the sedatives I had received in the ICU, my mood swinging without warning. Their visits confused me, and I was often silent with my own thoughts, making futile plans for my imminent departure from the hospital or lost in the fear that I might never leave. I could not recall what was said from one visit to the next, what requests I had made, and to whom. Family phoned, but I was often in therapy, unable to take their calls; or I was out of my room for checkups when they dropped in; or I was catching up on gossip with the new visitors and let the phone ring and forgot to return calls.

It was high time to leave the recovering, busy patient to himself.

"You're doing so much better now," Jean said.

"We can't visit as often," Karl announced. "Kate's moving her stuff to Montreal. Marie's overwhelmed with catching up at the two stores, and I'm finishing up a big cabinet for one of her clients."

"And Gary and I are going to be in Arizona visiting with Tosh," Jean said, and added, "She wants you to stay at her new house in Tucson when you feel better."

I nodded my head to everything, but I knew something important was not being said: Having stood by me during my darkest days and nights, they now needed some time away from me for their own recoveries. They wanted to get back to their own lives.

⁓

As I grew stronger, I also wanted to get back to my life as I had lived it before: I wanted to return to my writing. I phoned Mary Jo to see if she had edited the thirty-five pages that I had given to her just before I landed at St. Mike's.

"Can you bring those two chapters with you the next time you visit?"

"Only got through the first ten pages," she said. "School's started and I'm interviewing the new students and writing reports. I'm sorry—you know how it is."

I didn't. Usually we would go over my drafts within a few days of her having received them.

"But," she said, and laughed, "I can still visit you, can't I?"

"Of course."

I immediately took Mary Jo's hesitation as a sign: she had hesitated because those first pages were badly written; worse, she knew something about my medical condition and probably didn't want to tell me this novel would never be finished.

At the very beginning of our seventeen years of friendship, Mary Jo mocked my ideas about signs, of seeing and of interpreting them. "Survivors pay attention to signs," the pioneers of Old Chinatown had instilled in me: a door slamming shut on its own meant a ghost was present; money found on the sidewalk meant you would be lucky in the next fan-tan game; a stranger's portentous glance, your own ominous moods, your favourite insect or animal making a fortuitous appearance, all signalled your oncoming good or bad fate and required your attention. Taking notice of signs gave one the chance to turn things around, to mediate the randomness of life.

"I don't believe in signs, Wayson," Mary Jo told me. "Too New Age."

"Not *new* for at least a few thousand years," I said, "Not since clouds in the shape of dragons appeared before one of the Chinese emperors."

"If you haven't noticed," she said, laughing, "I'm not Chinese. I'm Irish."

"Amounts to the same thing," I said. "The Irish believe in luck, too. Haven't you ever bought a lottery ticket when you felt lucky?"

"Sure," she said, "even though the odds are crazy."

The odds *were* crazy, I agreed, but Mary Jo happened to be with me the second time I had felt what I called gut-lucky and bought tickets that won a thousand dollars here, a hundred dollars there, or, when feeling that way, I threw my name in a draw box. I had told her the time I went back to a particularly lucky store to buy two extra Wintario tickets because 7 was a lucky number and I had only purchased five tickets. That February evening in 1982, I'd just had a feeling I was lucky. Mary Jo smiled. She had heard this story before she met me.

"That's when you won a hundred thousand dollars."

"Right," I said. "Pay attention."

⌒

The moment Mary Jo stepped into my sunlit room, she distracted me with a paper bag. She made no mention of the locked doors she had just passed through, or my manuscript.

"Take it," she said.

The small package sat heavily in my palm.

"I think it's one of your signs. Open it."

From inside a wad of Chinese newspaper emerged a mottled-coloured dragon head, its neck coiling out of a shell-like body, a beautifully carved creature rising from its jade-dark base. The stone sculpture sat snugly in the palm of my hand like a paperweight. I thought of those unread, unedited pages.

"A sea dragon—can you see?—and it has the body of a turtle."

"And it's magnificent," I added.

She told me how she got the thing. Briskly walking down Yonge Street to the hospital, she passed an elderly Asian woman standing at an open kiosk hawking some curios. The woman stepped out and grabbed at her sleeve, tugging her backwards, and insisted she buy it.

"Bring good luck," she said to Mary Jo. "Bring good health."

"The old lady just hung on to me and insisted that I had to buy it. 'Bring someone good luck, bring someone good health'—she kept repeating this over and over—'You know someone *need* this, maybe someone ill,' and she kept dropping the price until I knew I had to get it for you. It's one of your signs, don't you think?"

I held up the dragon's head for a closer inspection. The tiny scales shimmered in the sunlight as if it were emerging from some invisible sea.

"Beautiful," I said. "The details are exquisite."

Another friend, Lynda, taking time off from her theatre troupe, had earlier brought me a braided bracelet of jade turtles. "For longevity," she told me. Now those linked turtles had a guardian sea dragon to keep them company.

"You're getting stronger, Wayson."

"I can sit up by myself."

I tried to pull myself up.

"Careful!" She took the dragon from my hand. "Hey, you're doing pretty well."

As my chest heaved with the effort, she averted her eyes a moment, then looked back at me to see whether I had made it or had collapsed. My torso was slumped crookedly over a pile of supporting pillows, my head barely higher. After exercising twenty minutes with the walker just before Mary Jo had arrived, I was happily as up as I could get. I pointed in the direction of the late-August sunlight. The metal walker glinted against the window ledge.

"Soon they'll have you jogging," Mary Jo laughed.

I grumbled about the macaroni, the peas, carrots, everything mashed up.

"Tonight"—my mouth bent at the corners, mouthing out the words—"I will eat with a fork and spoon. I want a steak knife. I want a steak."

Mary Jo looked so sympathetic I couldn't stop myself: "And I miss all my friends—you should see all the cards and notes. I might just cr—"

"We don't like maudlin, Wayson!" Mary Jo held the dragon in front of me.

I studied the jade-green carving. "Yes, a powerful sign," I said finally.

"You think? The old lady was like the Ancient Mariner grabbing at my sleeve and insisting I take it."

Mary Jo read my thoughts and smiled.

"I'm going to start working with you on those two last chapters of your novel, Wayson, the first day you're fully recovered." She gestured for me to open my palm. The mythic creature slipped from her fingers and found its home. "I promise you," she said.

Chapter 8

⁓

MY DISCONNECTED BRAIN MESSAGES—MY MOTOR MEMORY—
were now finding their way back to the right muscles: the more
I did, the more I practised, the more the messages travelling
from my brain were reconnecting with familiar pathways.

With a deep breath and deeper sigh, I finally stepped out on
my own into the wide, curving hallway. No trumpets sounded.
No one noticed or seemed to care. I lifted my walker, shuffling
past patients of every age, their eyes hollowed, their tongues
stilled. However unjust, their sad condition emboldened me to
work harder at my recovery. My arms and legs, fingers and toes
began to flex at my command. *I'm not you, not you*, I would think,
staring sadly at each broken being that I avoided bumping into
as if they were contagious. *I'm lucky to be me*, I said, over and
over again.

One day, a wretched-looking woman turned her head and
glared hard at me. I ignored her, attempted to lift my walker
past her. With a throaty horking sound, she spat at me. She
missed. For a second I wanted to lift up my walker and bean

her in the head. But she ran from me, and the nurse caught her spitting at another patient. Then the woman spat at the duty nurse. Spittle ran down the lovely face. No one did anything.

"Miss J., you mustn't do that," the woman in charge scolded, and quietly took Miss J. by the hand and walked her back to her room.

I counted to ten, then counted my blessings and walked on.

⁓

I kept walking. The cleaning staff gave me discreet thumbs-up; the nurses' assistants, encouraging smiles. In their ordinary and proud ways—the way some held their mops and pushed down hard; the way others balanced trays and rolled carts of laundry away; the way they all paid attention like silent foxes to everything and everyone around them—they reminded me of the elders of Old Chinatown who kept their pride, though they took on any work to feed their families.

Once, not paying attention to the little cramps groaning in my gut—signs, too, of course—I didn't make it to the toilet and did more than just wet the floor. Someone appeared with special towel-sized wipes, and another, just as quickly, showed up with a mop and bucket to clean up the mess.

"No worry, sir," said Martin with his musical English and "Cleaning Staff" stamped on his ID card. Martin had a genuine smile for everyone. He had the power to make even the most haughty medical specialists, however lost in his or her own prestige, pay attention to him and, reluctantly, smile back. His dark skin glowed and his Caribbean accent sang. "Can happen me, too."

A Taiwanese nurse, small and delicate in stature, came to wash me down. I was exhausted and had to sit naked and humiliated in a shower chair built like a toilet seat. The small woman held a hose that rained down on me, and then she bent down slightly and held the hose below so that the warm water splashed up against my testicles.

"Stand up, please, sir," she said. "Turn little this way."

I surrendered to her directions, wishing with all my heart that she did not have to observe with her young face, her lovely eyes, my withered body in the merciless glare of the shower lights.

I stared disheartened at the crumpled folds of my sunken tummy, once taut with youth. I remembered suddenly how as a boy of nine or ten, I had found a prize in a box of Cracker Jack. The memory made me look again at my body.

The prize was a small booklet of upside-down cartoon figures that were happy held one way and sad when turned the other. There was a Buddha who smiled at me when upright, and whom I hesitated to turn around. Observing the cartoon face my folds of skin made, I longed for a thick, black marker to draw some whiskers there, just below the belly-button nose; then I would stand on my head for the full effect: the whiskers would now become the toupee of my private Buddha face.

I wanted the young woman to join in my defensive joke and laugh with me. That's what I did when I was a child and the elders of Chinatown told me their funny stories and made wildly comic faces, I laughed with them. You laugh with old people.

Head bowed, I pointed at my tummy and caught the nurse's attention.

"See the belly-button nose," I said. "See the dimpled eyes—one here, the other there. Can you see this big smile?" Finally, I said, "Do you see Buddha?"

Instead of laughing, she pointed at my head. She said, "Buddha." She pointed at my heart and said, "Buddha." She tapped the washcloth on my belly and said, "Buddha." She pointed to my toes and said, "Buddha, Buddha . . . *all* Buddha."

She lowered her head, like someone bowing, but only slightly. She went on with scrubbing my back.

"Please, sir," she said, and handed me the facecloth. "You wash front."

She lifted the hose and aimed at my chest. Against the bright shower lights, the spray reflected back diamonds.

⁓

In bed, long after visiting hours, I would listen to the buzzer signalling late entrances and exits. One night, after a day of small victories, and with the full moon hanging over the top of the cathedral outside my window, I saw myself boldly getting off the bed, dressing myself in a fresh shirt, zipping up new trousers, and stepping into my best shoes. I could see myself strolling out and through those parting glass doors. At first, I was breathing easily with that happy image of my eyes looking for my reflected glory in those wide panes of plate glass. Then, without warning, I felt a tightness in my chest as I glimpsed a face that was not unlike my own, but with a deathly pallor, staring back at me. I reached for the puffer at my bedside. I breathed in a first, then a second blast of salbutamol, and my lungs opened up like dragon lungs. An old Chinatown saying came back to me: "When things go well, look behind you."

I hadn't looked, had wanted to ignore Miss J.'s fixed glare, and somewhere in the deepest part of her where she was still sane, she knew I had insulted her, and she spat at me.

The next time the family and Mary Jo were all together in my room, I told them how I was spat at, and then about the accident I had had in the hallway, and how everyone without complaint rushed to clean up both of our messes.

"Angels work here," Marie commented. "I'm not religious but I know angels when I see them."

"Michael was one of those angels, for sure," Mary Jo said.

"And Treasure," Karl said. "Treasure was wonderful."

I looked blankly at them. I couldn't remember Treasure at all.

I had trusted dozens of unseen hands, expert and ordinary, to deliver me from the dark. And what of all those unknown persons who handle the paperwork, the record keepers and accountants, what of those who clean and cook, wash and scrub, those who deal with the politics of running a hospital? I had been saved by invisible networks of compassion, by people who had borne untold difficulties and survived famines and wars and revolutions, to salvage the likes of me. I stood in my walker and stared at the nurses, orderlies, cleaning staff, and patients.

I took another step, then another and another.

My rapid progress encouraged the medical team to move me out of the lock-down facility. I was being transferred to a rehab hospital just three blocks from my Riverdale home. When I was being wheeled out to the ambulance, a group of patients, a few bent crookedly over their canes and walkers, stood around in their gowns to take in the unusual activity: someone dressed like them was departing in broad daylight.

Seven of them watched as I waved farewell; two tentatively waved back. The glass doors shut behind me.

Chapter 9

⎯⎯⌒

SHARING A SEMI-PRIVATE ROOM PERCHED A HALF MILE above the scenic Don Valley suited me perfectly: I loved watching the eight lanes of distant traffic and the nightly display of blinking headlights. At Riverdale Hospital, I was expected to regain the use of my legs and walk independently, undergoing months more of physiotherapy.

"You'll soon be walking home from here," the nurse told me. "You can almost see your house if you look out the windows at the end of the hall."

I had already looked a few times, and thought, *So near and yet so far* . . . I still didn't have the confidence to let go of the walker I had unwittingly come to depend upon, not only for physical support but, to be frank, for the sympathy of others. I could let go of the thing and walk about ten steps away from it and walk back only eight by myself. *Had I been counting on the dramatic "fall" towards the walker to make my visitors gasp, my therapist jump, my heart leap?* My friend Richard, who knew of stage craft—at parties he enjoyed himself costumed in glittering

Cantonese opera drag, or in eighteenth-century court dress, or in a nun's habit—watched this show twice and decided to call me on it. I had reached the eighth step and was, as expected, very shaky.

"Stop being a drama queen, Wayson," he said. His no-nonsense tone straightened my spine. "Just suck in your gut and take those last steps and get it over with. When I visit you next Monday, I want you to try thirty steps both ways and then throw that thing away. Thirty steps will take you to the elevators and the TV room, and thirty back will get you right into your room. I counted while you were busy playing the Matchstick Girl. Just do it."

I did.

But even Richard's encouragements could not improve my fine motor skills, which, for reasons the brain would not reveal to anyone, would not cooperate. I began dropping things again, clumsy in ways I hadn't been at St. Mike's. I still could not hold up a ballpoint pen and write my name clearly. Opened books slipped away from my fingers. I was easily exhausted again, suddenly tired for no reason, as if I were regressing. I told Richard.

"You're stressed out," he said. "I'll ask the Sisters to pray for you on this one. Race you to your room!"

Instead, I took his arm and we walked slowly back together.

Leo, my new roommate, ten years my senior and as distinguished looking as a model in a retirement ad, smiled to see my friend again. We three were comrades of the same orientation.

Leo had been a milliner in Yorkville during the Swinging Sixties. He ran a successful fashion house and retired with enough funds to buy a smart apartment on Avenue Road. One day, in his seventieth year, he tripped over a shag rug and fractured some major ankle and leg bones. After two botched operations, he lost the use of his legs. An electric wheelchair was parked next to his bed by the window. He kept a collection of old Hollywood classics on video by his side, and he would play them for me and my visitors at whim. A large rented TV hung above his bed. His shelf on the window held a Bible and some large-print novels. He loved Zane Grey.

"Wayson will be going home long before me," he said to Richard. "I'm glued to this bed."

"I think so, too," Richard said as he pulled the blanket up to my chin to keep out the chill from the air conditioner. "His Toronto family is getting his room ready for his homecoming. Lots of clutter. Ripley's *Believe It or Not* is going to—"

"Goodnight, Richard," I said.

I was too tired to think of the mess I had left behind in my former life.

⌒

Karl and Marie had consulted with the medical team about my going home. My living quarters would have to be stripped of dirt-trapping rugs, the attic room cleared of books, papers, old clothes—anything that attracted dust, dampness, pollen, or mildew.

"Will that be a problem for Mr. Choy?"

What Karl and Marie must have thought then. Twenty-five years' worth of my manic collections were piled high in and around twelve crammed bookcases and three desks; extra bedding and clothes were shoved under a double bed. It would be a Herculean excavation job: they would need a team of volunteers.

With his faithful Sheltie, Lilly, by his side, Ken, my personal assistant and official archivist, kicked into high gear, recruiting friends and coercing help. Even some of my students showed up—and left, no doubt, with fewer illusions about their teacher's elegant life. Our neighbour stood out on the sidewalk to investigate the commotion that was shaking his adjoining walls.

"Joe!" Karl shouted down to him. "We're going to find out where they buried Jimmy Hoffa!"

Taped boxes labelled BOOKS filled the basement from floor to ceiling. Ken tried his best to keep out of everyone's way while he frantically organized my papers for the archives. In the midst of labelling and packing my jumbled files and assorted letters, mementoes, and tapes, Ken was "fired" by a majority vote for slowing everyone down, but he persisted and secretly salvaged and labelled what he could, recognizing in every object and every scrap of paper my impulse to gather, to store, to keep.

Unsuspecting acquaintances who innocently dropped by were roped into joining the dozens of family and faithful friends who packed and lifted more than fifty liquor and thirty larger grocery boxes of books and wrapped treasures; they stuffed loads of clothing into garbage bags and carried everything down three flights of narrow stairs.

Kate phoned me from her residence at McGill, reporting how her dad had finally dismantled the dozen teak-veneered bookshelves, working from dusk to dawn, how a team of four, swearing a blue streak, lifted the shelving boards and not one but three makeshift desks down into the basement.

"I don't think some of those people will ever talk to you again," she said.

Richard helped at the house almost every day. He told me how Karl had wielded his axe, chopped up the oversized bed, hacked apart the second-hand sofa, and smashed up two night tables and some old chairs.

"What were you doing with *three* kitchen chairs piled on top of each other?" Richard's hand rose into the air above my hospital bed. "And all those boxes of fancy stationery and mismatched envelopes? Makes no sense."

I had had plans. I had expected to sand and refinish those dusty Goodwill chairs. I had meant to write a few thousand notes in fine calligraphy to all my friends and readers. In fact, I had dozens of collectible fountain pens as proof of my good intentions. Abundance meant possibility, meant that life held a future with a cleared desk, a sturdy chair, and the pleasure of some old-fashioned correspondence, of a neat pile of envelopes stamped with lovely images and special postage ready to be mailed. Those three pressback chairs with their oak-leaf design made me feel that each of my godchildren would one day proudly inherit one. Now, the thought of my good intentions, so invested in the things that were all being cleared out, tightened my chest.

Duty bound to tell me everything, Richard went on, and I envisioned the action as it happened: The back window rains down mattress stuffing and wood scraps, chipped coffee cups and bowls. An assortment of plush floor mats explodes into dust bombs. Wads of out-of-style sweaters, army-surplus coats pinned with peace symbols, denim jackets with embroidered slogans, bellbottom pants—all gleefully take flight into the open air. A few long-tailed shirts unravel in the breeze and drape over the backyard tree like flags of surrender.

For the grand finale, a shag rug with a red and orange bull's-eye that Marie thought I'd given away years ago slaps onto the deck. A pillar-thick atomic cloud rises into the late-autumn sky.

I sank back into the hospital bed like a defeated child.

"You were breathing in all that dust in your room," Richard said, his face darkened with concern. "I mean, *seriously.*"

I admitted that, in fact, I hadn't really noticed. *Seriously.* I shifted my head on the pillow. Richard bent down, curved his arm around my shoulder, and gently lifted. I sat up and took a swig of ice water. He lowered his voice to a conspiratorial whisper.

"Do you want to hear about the mummified mouse droppings?"

"No," I said. "Thank you."

But Richard wasn't deterred. He was determined to have me understand the enormous challenge that had driven family and friends to the proverbial edge.

"Wayson," he began, "you should know that everyone is going to lecture you. I'm not lining up for the privilege."

I shrugged. My mind was focused on all that I had lost.

"You should know," he repeated, "poor Karl finally had to hire a truck to take everything away from the back deck—a great big construction dumpster."

Did he actually say *dumpster?*

Centuries later, on the site of ancient suburban landfill, a curious hand will dig up my precious junk and wonder at the miniature plastic dinosaurs, the disjointed dolls, the dried-up pens, the rotted bits of clothing, matted rug ends, chipped remains of coffee cups, the eight-hundred-plus pencils that I bought from a fire sale. I imagined in some future time a furrow-browed anthropologist asking the polluted air: "Once upon a time these objects meant something to someone. But what? . . . And *why?*"

Good question.

I blame my Aunt Anne. She and Uncle Harry came to live with us when I was five. The night before Christmas I saw a bare tree in the living room and was told to watch what would happen when Santa Claus came. Mother and Father had told me nothing about his arrival.

I woke up to a decorated tree and layers of presents, a big red wagon filled to overflowing, a toy rifle jutting out among boxed board games, a cowboy outfit with a cowboy hat just for me, trucks, and miniatures of animals and soldiers and . . . and more laughter and smiles poured over me than ever at my birthday parties. The joy of abundance.

I blame Santa Claus.

Chapter 10

⁓

THE MORNING OF SEPTEMBER 11, 2001, I LAY WITH EYES
shut against the light streaming in from the windows. In bed,
with my breakfast half eaten, I groggily got ready to face another
day in hospital.

I was bored. I wanted a quick recovery. What recovery I had
was *extremely slow.* Carol had repeatedly reminded my therapy
group of five that our "nothing-is-happening-to-me" days contained mounting successes. To that end, I had been introduced
to mat exercises, to lie on my back and rhythmically raise and
lower my legs and arms with one- and two-pound weights
strapped to them. All five of us, bit by bit, had charted important improvements. "Measurable," Carol would emphasize,
calling out numbers from her notes. Digits and limbs were
flexing; joints and reflexes responding; neck muscles strength-
ening. Two of us in the group were now using our breakfast
utensils without dropping them. Carol's assistant noted that two
of us could now curl our toes around a pencil-thin rod for five
to ten *measurable* seconds.

My fingers were still unable to grasp a pen, to propel its point across the paper, releasing the sentences from my head. I hadn't dared try my fingers on the keyboard in the reading room. What if I failed? But my toes could curl around the rod and hold on for at least five seconds. Toes were like digits. There was hope.

I glanced over at Leo for some conversation about our progress, but he was busy adjusting his earphones to watch a morning talk show. He had no trouble flexing or moving anything from his ankles up. "Don't give up on your toes," I wanted to say to him, as he himself had cheered me on during those first days. He kept fidgeting with the remote. I slumped my head back down onto the pillow and rolled over to face the open door.

Breakfast time was almost over. From the adjoining East Wing hallway, Rosie's trolley, loaded with empty water thermoses and dish-filled trays, rattled louder and louder.

"You done wit' foot?" Rosie's call into four- and six-bed rooms echoed closer to my ears. In a few minutes, she would poke her head in and alert Leo and me, "Ex-ah-cues please!"

I still had enough time to fuss over what to do with the remains of my breakfast. I sat up and tried to eat a little more. Rosie frowned at leftovers.

The hospital schedule was now routine to me: first pills would show up at 7:30; breakfast was served around 8:00, and Rosie usually reached Leo and me in the semi-private West Wing around 9:00. Showers were usually taken before 11:00. The digital travel alarm on my bedside table indicated the hour and minute, and in case I ever felt the need to count them, the seconds. Leo was content to use his TV schedule and his favourite shows—like "The Today Show" at 9:30—to mark the time.

I swallowed one more spoonful of the milky sludge piled in the cereal bowl.

"Eat more fibre," the nurse had said to me earlier that morning after watching me down my pills. "We need a bowel movement from you."

Truth was, I didn't have the same appetite I'd had when I left St. Mike's ten days before. Perhaps because of the stress of leaving the old and having to adapt to this new environment, the changes in routine, my mind crashing about with this worry and that, and not least that I was feeling well enough to indulge in my tendencies to deny or exaggerate future opportunities— or the lack of them, whatever the reason, I had slipped back into my usual bone-lazy nature. I just wanted to stay in bed and sleep the whole day.

I hadn't really done all the range-of-motion exercises assigned to me, so I hadn't worked up any appetite. My printed schedule dictated that I should do a wake-up regimen of movements, starting at my head and continuing all the way down to my toes. Eat breakfast. Repeat list. I did the list in my fashion: I wiggled my toes to stop the morning itches; a few slow neck turns did happen as I glanced from the breakfast tray to the sunlit windows.

I indulged in the idea that the imagination was a vital healing force: only *think* you're well, and you'll get better.

I went one step further.

Think exercise, I told myself. *Think of doing the most rigorous kinds, and you're on your way to one day doing them.*

"Keep track of how you're moving your body," instructed Joe, the physiotherapist who consulted with me the second day I was here.

"Keep track?"

"Yes." His tanned biceps bulged each time he lifted his pencil to make a point.

"Keep track of what, Joe?"

"Keep a mental diary. Keep a count of your physical routines. How many times do you get in and out of bed? Are you feeling stronger pushing yourself off to the side of the mattress? Do you still need much help to go to the bathroom?"

He went on, listing uncountable ways one could track bodily movement. I liked the distraction of his jaws moving, and the way he pointed to different parts of his own body. I gave him my most attentive smile, and wondered what kind of gel he used in his blondish hair. His blue eyes and sculptured features reminded me of Paul Newman in *Cat on a Hot Tin Roof*; his baritone voice lulled me. My libido, somewhat dormant for so long and nearly forgotten, was doing fine.

"And Mr. Choy, please take note if you still need a little or a lot of assistance putting on your socks. What about the shower? Do you move steadily there?"

I nodded, and for another delicious moment wondered how he himself, all six-foot-two of him, would look in the shower, the water splashing off those broad shoulders.

The new nurse went past us, a second and a third time, to stare at him, open mouthed. I envied her. She was pretty enough to turn his head. He did turn his head. Twice. Then back to me.

"And did you use the walker today, Mr. Choy? Are you holding on to the rail in the hallway? How's your grip? That's all exercise, and it *all* counts."

"Great, Joe," I said. "Thank you."

How sensible, I thought. I beamed, satisfied that, although only twenty percent of his words meant something to me, I had at least caught the gist of his lecture. He took my hand in both of his, not letting go.

"I know who you are, Mr. Choy," he said. "I've loved *The Jade Peony* ever since we took it in high school."

"That must have been a few years ago," I said, warmed by his unexpected smile. "You still remember my work?"

"Definitely," he said. "In class, I got caught up in a debate about that boxer kid."

"You did?"

"Yeah, because someone said a boxer couldn't be a fag. I said that even a jock could be a fag."

I took a chance: "Like you?"

"Some of them got that idea."

I laughed. "And you didn't mind?"

"Not at all, Mr. Choy."

"Please, feel free to call me Wayson."

"Wayson."

Joe gripped my hand a little tighter, it didn't matter why. He rushed away to catch up to the pretty nurse. I heard him say to her, "That guy is a writer."

⌒

As I was lying in bed that morning, still inspired by Joe's honest sense of goodwill, I repeated his words and began to concentrate on my fingers, pushing them to dance, to exercise, to open the tiny plastic packet of Kraft jam. I knew I had opened many of those packets before, but for some reason, I couldn't get my brain and my fingers together to cooperate. I didn't panic; I knew it would come back to me, as everything else had. Some things just took longer.

Days before, Leo had demonstrated the correct technique: (1) locate the minuscule tab—which I only had to pick at for five minutes to discover that it actually existed; (2) pull this tab back until the top peeled away; (3) remove jam with knife!

But I found it more efficient to stab the damn packet with a fork, squeeze the thing. Gobs of jam oozed onto the toast. The whole procedure punctuated with little fairy farts.

With my back facing him and with my eyes closed, I listened to the movements from my neighbour's bed. I knew that Leo was a morning person, waking before the sun rose, getting himself ready to exercise his damaged legs, to shift them off the bed, and to spend another day—mostly back in bed.

I could hear him moving about behind me, raising his bed with the lever and managing to sit himself up against a pile of pillows. Then he would carefully arrange his kingdom of water thermos, cup, tissue and chocolate boxes, magazines, and blue plastic urine bottle. Rosie always crinkled her forehead, narrowed her eyes, and shook her head at our two piled-up bed tables. On mine, there were a half-dozen books and well-intentioned blank notebooks, magazines, get-well cards and letters, a box of tissues, a pencil case, stationery, ink bottles (blue and red ink), and a turtle bracelet draped over a carved sea dragon.

"Wayson?" Leo's voice was very soft, tentative, directed at my back.

We had established an understanding, like congenial prisoners in a shared cell: To see our backs meant *Do not disturb—Dozing, Thinking, or Want to be left alone.*

His voice came at me again and pulled me away from my deliberations about the possibility of actually exercising.

"Wayson?" The grave voice rose from a half whisper to a final wake-up volume. "*Wayson!*" He saw me stir. "Wayson, please *do* look at the television screen."

I turned my body to face Leo's side and stared at the twenty-inch set that hung from the wall above the foot of his bed.

On the screen, across a clear, blue sky, a trail of something like smoke drifted from the middle of what might be a wide chimney or a building.

"Leo, what are we looking at?"

I focused my eyes and made out a pattern of structural ribs and rectangular windows.

"It's the World Trade Center in New York." Leo's voice registered the event like a news flash. "A plane just crashed into the North Tower."

"A private plane?"

"Probably. Can't imagine a commercial pilot would make this kind of mistake."

Leo and I watched, shaking our heads, tongues clucking in unison like members of a Greek chorus. Thickening dark clouds coiled and then began to billow out across the empty sky.

The camera pulled back. The skyline of New York and the two towers were now visible. Leo turned up the sound. The announcer sounded as if he was starting to panic.

"How could any trained pilot not see the tower?" I asked.

I swallowed. I attempted to take a deep breath to push aside the nightmare images of people trapped on the upper floors, watching the plane coming towards them. I choked and picked up my puffer and inhaled.

I said, "Maybe the plane had—had a mechanical failure."

"Maybe the pilot had a heart attack," Leo said, "and lost control."

"You're right," I said. "Someone I knew had a cousin who crashed his car during a heart attack. A mess."

During the minutes we had been transfixed by the glowing screen, the pick-up trolley reached our room. "Ex-ah-cues please!" I turned to push my bed table away from my side so that Rosie could collect my tray and the used dishes.

"No hungry?" she gently asked me. "I leave to you toast and jam?"

"No, thanks, Rosie. Not this morning."

The small woman shrugged and picked up my tray and reached over for Leo's tray, without looking up to see what Leo was staring at. Leo was too absorbed to smile back at her.

"Look, Rosie," I said, pointing to the TV. "It's in New York."

Her smile disappeared.

"A plane—" Leo began to explain.

My God! A woman's voice shot out from the TV. *My God! Oh my God!*

Leo turned up the volume. Screams and shouts shook our hospital room. A second voice jumped out from the speakers: *Another plane! It's another plane coming!*

The three of us saw the clear outline of a huge plane as it dove directly into the second tower, expanding into a ball of black smoke and white heat. From the sides of the pristine

South Tower, another fireball exploded.

I noted the time on my travel alarm: a few minutes after nine. Leo broke the silence. "What's happening?"

"Crazy," Rosie said, her voice rising in anger. "Some people crazy." After a moment, she gasped, her arms shook, and her eyes darkened. She grabbed for our two trays, the dishes bouncing, and rushed out of the room. Later she would recount for me stories of her youth in Vietnam: the slaughter she never forgot, and the two bombs she witnessed falling, and I saw in her eyes the flesh-clinging napalm raining down on her brother and two sisters, the balls of flames rising from her village. Rosie had known at once what was happening in New York.

Leo muted the TV. In the silence, I listened to my own breathing and heard the wheels of Rosie's trolley squeak and rattle down the hallway. Voices outside our room called to each other to rush to a television set. I heard someone shout, "Rosie! Rosie, slow down!"

Chapter 11

⌒

AFTER MORE THAN A MONTH AND A HALF IN THERAPY AT Riverdale Hospital, I no longer held on to the wall rails and no longer needed Richard's arm for balance. Now I could walk briskly. Zipping open packets of jam was nothing to me. The days and weeks after the terrorist attacks in New York had given me cause to scale my own problems down to size and wake up my brain cells. I picked up my pen, a dollar-store ballpoint, made notes, wrote cards of thanks and asked Ken to mail them for me. I was more mobile, but not yet ready to get back into my life as I had lived it before.

Would I ever be a writer or teacher again?

Move on, I told myself. *Climb one tiny hill at a time. Everest can wait. Just walk out of here on your own two feet first.*

I simplified my goals to achieve one small thing every hour, every day. I refused to worry about the future. I thought often of those who had lost their lives on 9/11 and those who had suffered the senseless loss of loved ones. I thought even of the deaths of those who had aimed the planes, each of them ensnarled by their youthful ideals and their wilful intent to kill, all committed for the better day they, too, dreamed would come. And I saw clearly then that the future, even as I might dream to have it, might never arrive.

So, I reasoned, what can I do today? This hour? This moment? What other gifts do the gods grant us except these few precious seconds ahead of our next deep breath?

I paid attention.

Carol expertly taught me to focus on a body I had neglected. (Joe had, alas, been assigned to another floor.) She taught me again to pay attention to muscle tone, recovery time, pay attention to time-outs, and to let my brain connections and my muscles track their paths without any more neurotic interferences about the future. I took in ninety percent of everything she said.

Riverdale had a beautiful patio garden, surrounded by a high brick wall, lovingly planted by volunteers with trees and hanging plants around a pool of goldfish and tiny turtles. I spent hours there, under a table umbrella, reading, watching the turtles climb up onto little rocks to sun themselves or settle in to absorb the glint of gold scales that swished about, and then vanish into the depths of the pool like gilt-brushed calligraphy.

I walked everywhere on the hospital grounds, never rushed, barely noting the distant Don Valley traffic rushing back and forth, and I thought of nothing more than how these days of rest and careful exercise were a gift. The first small hill was climbed, then a second, and a third even higher, and then another. I was walking entirely on my own, climbing stairs, using the handrails, always stepping carefully, and sometimes I was propelled by images of those stairs in the Twin Towers smothered in black smoke and screams before their final collapse. How terrible to be pushed by that tragedy to move on; yet through those days of recovery, every thought of darkness rendered to me some kind of light that moved me forward.

One sunny October day, Carol and the medical team gave me permission—"If you'd like to, Mr. Choy"—to walk the three blocks home, "for an afternoon break."

Marie brought me a fresh set of street clothes, my favourite sweater, and a new coat to guard against the October winds. I dressed myself while she helped me to tie my shoes. I walked down the hall on Marie's arm, not for support but for the blessing of her company. We took the elevator and walked out towards Broadview, and started home.

I savoured each slow step. Along the two blocks towards our Victorian brick house, the shadow-strewn trees glowed with autumn colours. The fall air smelled of cool, damp earth. Winter was coming, but to paraphrase Camus' words, I felt some kind of eternal summer lingering in the air.

Finally, Marie put the key in our front door and stepped aside. I pushed it open. Belle sat waiting in the front hall. She hadn't been fed and was watching for anyone who might walk in and open a can of victuals. It was good to see that Belle was just the same.

"Hi, Belle," I said.

She got up, strutted in the direction of her empty food dish, in case I thought that I had any other priorities.

I sat at the kitchen table to rest a moment. Marie called Karl out of the back workshop to join us, and I remembered that Kate was finishing her fall term at McGill.

"It's so good to be sitting here," I said, "if only for this afternoon."

"Nice to have you sitting here, Wayson."

Belle meowed at Karl as he walked in. Ignoring her, he came over and gave me a hug.

"Can you have coffee?" he asked.

"Yes, if you make it."

"What do you think?" Marie said, and they laughed together.

Karl said, "You think we want *you* to make it and poison us?"

Marie touched my hand. "Want to see your room while the coffee's brewing?"

I was ready. Sort of. My stomach churned. Thinking of my collecting compulsion, I couldn't help feeling a little repentant as well. I had to stay calm. But first, I decided to open a tin of Fancy Feast for my four-legged pal while Karl was filling the coffee pot. I reached up and opened the cupboard for a tin. Karl tried to take it from me.

"Let me," I said, and took the can opener out. I had been using my hands very efficiently. Had even hand-written a note with a fountain pen, a note to the doctor about changing a scheduled blood test—and each word was clearly *printed*, unlike those scrawled note cards I sent that provoked some friends to phone and ask me if I had taken up fingerpainting or had gone blind. Leo said I should have my agent reproduce the doctor's note in *Maclean's* magazine, just to remind my few readers I was still alive and *printing*.

I fumbled with the can opener. I knelt down beside Belle. The food slopped out into the tiny dish, and her moist nose immediately, rudely, shoved my hand aside. I rudely shoved back, patted her on the head, and slowly stood up. Belle's tail thrust up into the air. I thought of the demon Fox Lady's tail as she happily crunched on the boiled flesh and bones of disobedient, careless children.

"I'm ready to see my old kingdom in the sky," I said.

I pushed myself off the chair and we walked steadily to the front-hall staircase, the same stairs I had almost tumbled down on that August day when things started to go wrong with my lungs and heart.

With Marie in front of me and Karl behind, I climbed the last narrow, walled-in step to my room. I inhaled deeply and held my breath. I turned my head to look at my once-familiar digs. My crammed beehive had disappeared. The place now seemed—cavernously, echoingly—*empty*.

For the first time in almost twenty years I could see painted white walls. Bare walls. No pictures. No posters. No bulletin boards. Everything was gone. The room was hollow. Sterile. A few bundled flats of hardwood tiles sat like tiny pyramids in the centre of the room. Paint tins and wash pails were lined up along one wall. In the far corner, curtain rods wrapped in beige drapery stood at attention like distant soldiers. Half the uncovered expanse of floor gleamed with a skin of contact glue. Not a speck of dust in sight.

"The floor will be a natural oak," Karl said. His voice echoed in the room. "Nadine's been helping with sanding and painting the walls. People have been saints."

"Before they finish with you at Riverdale," Marie said, with the practised sweep of her decorator's arm, "we will have entirely redone your room."

Lingering glue and paint fumes began to choke me. We descended the stairs, Karl in front of me, Marie behind.

I knew that scores of strained backs and exhausted arms had worked for weeks. Afterwards, each member of the team, by phone, mail, or in person, swore to me that I was toast if I went back to my old ways. Jean and Gary gently reminded me of our friend Bob, who had once stayed a night in my room in Caledon and remarked the next day, "I just love the first ten of everything Wayson collects."

I insisted that Marie and Karl let me walk the two blocks back to the hospital by myself. Belle slipped away as soon as I opened the door. It was windy. Marie buttoned up my coat.

"Walking back by myself," I said, "that'll build up my confidence."

They didn't argue.

~

I scrawled in my notebook: *4:15 p.m. Just got back. Slipped out of street clothes and back into hospital gown. Settled in for dinner and some small talk with Leo. Eyes beginning to water. . . .*

My mind began to fill with the chaos of stuff that I had once owned. I put the pen down. I was going to have to face a future stripped of objects from the past, of mementoes symbolic of people and times, and now left only in my memory. Had the totality of my things meant so little to those who loved me?

I must have seemed a little lost to Leo. He knew that I would be seeing my attic room again for the first time, and he had heard all about the cleaning and hauling and sorting and . . .

Hadn't he gone through this, too, the loss of all his collections, his furnishings, everything movable taken out from his Avenue Road apartment? He had, and I had not paid serious attention to the pain in his voice when he told me of the auction and the antique dealers who bid low for his paintings and silverware, and the friends who claimed his belongings . . .

"Hello, Leo," I said. "I don't mean to lie here and say nothing to you." I began to sniff a bit. A runny nose. Autumn pollen.

From his bedside chair, peering over his reading glasses, my roommate asked, "Anything wrong, Wayson?"

"I just saw my place," I said, dabbing my eyes. "It's completely empty. They're just redoing my floors . . . repainting . . ."

"Of course," Leo whispered. He tossed me his box of tissues. "I do understand. It must be the paint fumes."

⁓

Ten days later, while a gust of autumn wind rattled the windows, I tried to say goodbye to everyone at Riverdale. Rosie had gone back home to Vietnam with gifts for her family and so missed my leaving. Some of the staff had brought copies of my books for me to autograph. I signed with a flourish, my writing hand magically in full strength again. At the last hour, Carol came and told me how I was one of her best successes and that she didn't want to see me back in Riverdale as a patient again. Leo gave me an alpaca coat he had designed for himself in his salad days: it hung on me like a robe and almost touched the floor. The tawny material made me feel I was the Lion King—or wearing him.

"Wayson," Leo said, shaking my hand, "you'll be glam for winter."

Karl came, greeted Leo, saw the coat draped about my shoulders but made no mention of it. "Are you ready to go home? Where's your suitcase?" He hustled me out of the room.

In the elevator he asked, "What's it feel like to be leaving this place?"

"Feels good," I said. "I don't want to come back, that's for sure."

"What are you going to do with that coat?" Karl said, no doubt remembering all the piles of clothing that he had thrown out from my room.

"Not sure," I said, sensing the early beginnings of a tug-of-war. The coat might have been a sign, at least for Karl. "What's for supper?"

"Steak and corn on the cob."

I was home.

⌒

That first night Marie told me to leave my bedroom door wide open, in case I needed to call out to them.

"We'll keep our door open, too," she said. "Less worry for us."

Back in my own bed, a deep sense of guilt invaded my sleep. Tossing and turning, I saw faces breathing through swirling grey clouds clearing out my room, arms straining to gather and pile and throw, faces twisted with frustration at my longing for more and more things. I saw myself humbled and repentant, monk-like, in a room emptied of everything but a single bed and a dangling lamp.

I awoke peering above the new sheers. I saw the full moon caught between bare branches and I could not help myself—I smiled at how well I was loved.

A few hills still left, I heard myself whisper and lowered my eyes.

Belle sat patiently by my bed looking as if she were waiting for me to say something.

"I want *more,*" I whispered, "more of everything."

THREE

"One world at a time."

—Henry David Thoreau

Chapter 12

⟳

WITH EVERYTHING THAT HAD BEEN DONE FOR ME BY MY
extended family and friends, I was determined to be in charge
of my life again. With his usual thoughtfulness, Karl had put
up a sturdy banister so that I could safely go up and down that
final staircase with confidence. A plastic chair sat waiting for
me in the shower. I could now push back any thoughts of past
dangers and start celebrating my recuperation and recovery. For
those final two months of 2001, as an outpatient of the hospital, I kept to the tight schedule of appointments.

"You'd better," said Karl.

I was a perfect rehab outpatient. I attended every one of the
sessions designed to build up my strength and increase my
motor skills. One of the hospital therapists called me a trooper
for the extra effort I put into our take-home exercise sheets.

Flowers, chocolates, and get-well cards and letters arrived at
the house welcoming me back, and a huge bouquet of fruit-
sculptured flowers came with a lovely note from my ever-patient
publisher. Each encouraging gesture from my friends—the

candles Walt and Berenice lit in church alcoves, the Eagles' prayers for my pagan soul, the Hungarian chicken soup from Margaret, those herbal broths from Tony and Evelyn, and pots of broth from Irish Michael brewed from his Chinese mother-in-law's recipe —helped me to get back to familiar routines. Like reading a dozen newspapers and magazines to catch up and doing some writing on the computer. Folding my laundry. Cooking for myself. Eating out. A little shopping at the local mall. Driving my Toyota again.

I soon took to driving away from the house in all kinds of wintry weather—against Karl's advice. Eager for the good company I missed so much, I went dining with friends and stayed late at their gatherings and celebrated the New Year.

"Wow," I said to everyone, at least two or three times at every occasion. "I could have *missed* all this!"

At the slightest sound of my wheezing or coughing, caring companions who took me out—guardians all—would urge me to rest a moment or use my puffer.

"Still too skinny," Kate commented when she came home for a weekend. Her bluntness convinced me I was looking much better. One could never be too thin.

I went to see *Lord of the Rings* with Mary Jo and sang out repeatedly my mantra of gratitude. "Wow," I said, my eyes drinking in that mountainous terrain, "I could have *missed* all this!"

"Shuuuuut up," Mary Jo whispered.

"Shhhhhhh . . ." hissed Frodo from the screen.

Suddenly, sword-waving, hooded creatures on wild steeds thundered into view. I felt truly alive and happy.

In January of 2002, almost six months after my trauma, I went back to Humber teaching one English class a week. I stayed focused on the healthy-eating plan drawn up by the nutritionist, and received approval to fly to Vancouver when *The Jade Peony* was selected as "the book to read" for the entire city. I was busy making plans and busy writing in circles, busy accepting invitations and making appointments and wanting to teach more classes. Being busy assured the spinning wheels in my head that I was back in charge and fully alive again.

I was exhausted, joyously in denial.

For the first two weeks after I was back from Vancouver, I found myself napping more than I had ever needed to: at least three times a day. I took my naps secretly, so that the household would be spared the trouble of worrying about me. After all, I was on a roll, and only needed a little rest now and again.

To the queries from Dr. David about my time in Vancouver and how I managed to keep up, I answered proudly, "Did it all, David," and beamed with satisfaction.

To the good doctor's thoughtful questions about my mental state, I chose not to bother him with mention of the sudden hallucinations I still had to shake off, like the uninvited visit from the Queen of Water one night. Instead, I joked that I was no crazier than before. I told David what one of the Riverdale team had said to me about my brain cells, after I had passed a final series of tests for memory and verbal dexterity: "Congratulations, Mr. Choy. It looks like all your faults are intact."

New stuff, *things,* began to occupy my attic room. I begged Karl to replace some of my bookcases. He allowed me two. The shelves filled up quickly, and stacks of books began to multiply on the floor. Ken had saved most of my research files and notes for my novel and stored them in grocery cartons in the basement. I brought them back upstairs, along with boxes of stationery and gift wrap that I had to have. I discovered that much that I had treasured had been neatly put away in a storage locker. I went by stealth and hauled back up to my room the most missed treasures: three cartons of books on the art, philosophy, and history of Old China.

After I looked around for someplace to put down the last carton, the phone rang. A little breathless, I sat down and waited a moment before answering. It was Denise, my agent.

"What's wrong?" she asked.

"Nothing, just moving some things around."

"You sound winded."

"Trust me," I said, "I'm fine."

"Will you be fine enough to fly to China in five weeks?"

⁓

The chance to go to China to host a documentary film about Confucius had first been offered to me a year before. I was thrilled that the invitation had been offered again. As a boy of six I had stubbornly declared in Chinglish, "I belong Canada." The elders had thrown back, "You Chinese!"

"One day you go back China," a few had told me then. "You see you belong China."

"Chinese is best," the elders insisted. All my life, I had wondered whose conviction was right, theirs or mine. In the 1960s, I had fought against the American government's refusal to give me a green card because they had already had enough "Chinese" applicants; I had demanded that Prime Minister Pearson stand up in Parliament and unequivocally defend my Canadian-born citizenship. My conviction that I was Canadian, that I belonged to Canada, had remained unshaken all these years. But maybe the elders knew more about being Chinese than I had ever accepted. I had never been on Chinese soil; I had never breathed Chinese air.

It was easy enough to be Canadian, perhaps, when I had only ever been in Canada. And still among my collection of things was a disproportionate number of things Chinese—pieces of jade, paintings, carvings, calligraphy scrolls, fans. I had even taught myself brush painting and a bit of calligraphy. Cartons of books on the old country, a collection started when I was sixteen, had followed me around since. My rooms in Jean and Gary's country home held shelves of China books, many written by missionaries. More were stored in cartons in the homes of relatives and friends in Vancouver. No, I had not read them all, but their pages waited for me, warehoused like dormant memories. When I was finally ready, they seeded the research for my stories of Chinatown.

Writing those stories, I felt more Chinese. I would look in the mirror and see a Chinese face. Some days I relished the romance of being the heir to thousands of years of history. And now here was the opportunity to wander in the same fields and hills that Confucius once did. Maybe in those fields and hills, with that land under my feet, I would feel finally what I had never felt before—that I belonged to China.

When the film offer first arose, I had prepared for the assignment by reading all about Confucius. I searched my memory for the many times my father quoted the philosopher's sayings. I wanted to trace how Confucian ideas like the golden rule, the emphasis on filial obedience and on worshipful respect for one's ancestry, were woven throughout my family life and as conflicted themes in my stories. That July, almost a year after making the offer, the film company faxed the contract for my signature. I told my Toronto family the exciting news.

"Before you sign and fly away," Marie insisted, "check with Dr. David."

"Eighteen hours of cabin pressure," Karl warned, "can't be too good for people with heart conditions."

I asked the advice of the heart-and-lung specialists assigned to me during my long months of rehab at Riverdale. They each looked over a sheaf of reports on my progress. I was given some more tests. I passed them all. The cardiologist was especially pleased with the results.

"You shouldn't have any trouble on that overseas flight," he assured me. "But you're not going on one of those frantic ten-city tours, are you?"

"No," I said, sounding like a seasoned tourist. "I'll just be staying in one small town in Shantung province."

"Where?"

"Qufu," I said. "I'll have twelve days to explore the ancient hometown of Confucius."

How wonderful for you to visit your family's home country, one after another told me. *You'll see what it means to be part of such a proud heritage. You'll discover your roots! Get back to see your true history, know what it means to be Chinese!*

I didn't mention to any of the medical team that I was going to take part in ten compressed days of filming. The good doctor handed over a list of pills that I would need to cover my time in China.

At my next office appointment, I turned the list over to Dr. David and told him my plans for August. He gave me a box of surgical masks.

"In case," he said. "Where will they be filming you?"

"Mostly in the countryside and around the Confucian Temple Park in Qufu."

David added to the list five more emergency pills to alleviate infections or stomach problems, and to neutralize any unexpected hyperallergic reactions just in case there was a delay getting some medical attention.

"Imagine," David said. "You'll get a fresh look at all that ancient history. I envy you."

At the drugstore, checking over the total number of pills, I also read for the first time the long list of possible side effects: gas pains, rash, cramps in muscles and joints, various "rare" liver and kidney reactions, distorted vision, internal bleeding . . . Over the phone, I worriedly recited the list of short- and long-term effects to David.

"Wayson," he interrupted. "You have to die of *some*thing."

During the stopover in Vancouver to change to the flight to Beijing, I went over the latest version of the shooting script with Trevor, the director, a man of quick insight and judgement.

"Don't fuss too much about those changes," he said as we boarded the plane. "No documentary script is set in cement. Too many things can happen. Just remember to be yourself in front of that camera."

Which self, I wondered, the peel or the banana? Trevor saw the puzzlement in my face.

"Stick to the main story," he said, helping me stow my carry-on bags above my cattle-class seat. "You're the writer looking through two thousand years of myths, searching for Confucius the man, not just the legend that had all that influence on your Chinese family."

I appreciated that storyline. Confucius's sayings, his wisdom and philosophy, had deeply influenced the way Chinatown raised first sons like me.

What kind of human being was he to have established as one of the tenets of his philosophy, "What you do not want done to yourself, do not do to others"? How different the assumption that our fear of how others can harm us is the most specific and universal deterrent compared to what has filtered down to Western culture as "Do unto others what you would have them do unto you." How dangerous to assume that whatever pleases you might please me. None of his teachings ever touched upon the afterlife, none considered the possibilities of a heaven or hell. His concern was with how one might live life in the present. Having survived my almost dying, I was moved by the answer he offered when one of his followers, speaking of death, asked, "But what comes next?"

Confucius said, "If you do not understand life, how will you know about death?"

When I read that, I saw a man free to live his life fully, making no bargains with men or gods.

I loved the poetry of his thoughts, appearing as naturally as inked images on scrolls. Those in power were like the wind, and the people were like a sea of grass bending towards good or evil with the leader's example. He held the powerful accountable and was targeted for assassination by one of them. The assassin paused to listen to the Old Master teaching his disciples and he put away his dagger.

I had a thick set of notes on the philosopher and his life, and had already gone over all my lines in the script. In order to be *me*, I had altered the rhythm and phrasing of sentences to match my own speaking voice.

"I have absolute confidence in you," Trevor said, eyeing me with his pale eyes—were they grey or green?—as he patted my shoulder and then strode away into business class.

My English-speaking Chinese seatmate, a businessman with a recently acquired Canadian passport, told me how happy he always was to fly back to China and be at home again with his family.

"You visiting your family, too?" he asked me.

"Sort of," I said. "But I was born in Canada. This is my first trip to Beijing and—"

"Oh yes, but one is always Chinese," he rushed to assure me, "no matter where you are born," and echoed the voices of Old

Chinatown. "Once you see China, the great beauty of old things in the homeland, you'll understand, you'll be very proud you are Chinese."

I was meant to be finished my filmed part within the first seven days and was promised two or three days of vacation time in Beijing. I would soon stand before "old things," the treasures, the writings, and the buildings dating back thousands of years.

I knew from my Internet research that Gobi Desert winds now and again swept across the capital to churn the polluted air into a mixture of yellowish gritty microparticles that choked lungs and rubbed them raw, microparticles that were gradually microdissolving the patina and paintings on ancient temples. *Dust to dust,* I thought, *old or new, that's what all things come to.*

I had all my medications in my carry-on, four inhalers, and a dozen surgical masks to fight off the bad air of China. I arched my back against the rigid seat, imagined myself climbing along the Great Wall, puffer at the ready if the Gobi whipped up a sandstorm. I revelled in the idea that I would be tracing the steps of the great Kublai Khan and all the fabled emperors of China. If I died in China, would I want to have my ashes scattered there? Did others wonder about such things? The thought irritated me, as if the question should matter to anyone at all. Dead is dead. I was comforted by the fact that Confucius focused on living.

My friend Elaine would be in Beijing to introduce me to her cousin, an expert guide who promised to open the Forbidden City Gate an hour earlier to sneak us in. I would glimpse things that, as far as I knew, my mother and father had never seen, and that I had only imagined from the Cantonese operas of my childhood or seen in epic movies like *The Last Emperor*, or in those lush National Geographic documentaries. I shut my eyes to blank out the kung-fu movie showing on the screen in front of me, Jackie Chan battling the bad guys in what looked like New York.

"Wait until you see the throne room," Elaine had said to me back in Toronto. "We'll be the only ones there."

Perhaps my bloodline was a link back to some imperial household, or even back to Confucius himself? I took a deep breath, felt for the emergency puffer in my shirt pocket, and opened my eyes. Jackie Chan hollered, slammed his fist into the air, and cracked someone's jaw; he leapt and swung his fist again.

I shut my eyes.

The plane roared through the night. Half asleep, I began daydreaming of food. I imagined all the rich Chinese delicacies waiting for me in fancy restaurants and floating pavilions; the plates of stir-fry, dim sum savouries, the fish leaping from ponds into giant woks. As the varieties of unmentionable meats and bowls of exotic soups drifted by me, I breathed in their rich aromas. I was ready to jump off the low-fat diet wagon when an inviting voice stopped me: "Sandwich? Cup of noodles?"

The flight attendant paused her snack wagon right next to me and handed me a one-page menu. Tea—Chinese or English. Coffee. A soft drink. Not much choice in sandwiches—ham and cheese, egg salad, roast beef. I selected the Japanese instant noodles, handed over two toonies, and was told to keep the cup tightly lidded for at least two minutes. Impatiently tap-tapping the Styrofoam cup with the prongs of the white plastic fork, I wondered what Trevor, comfortably in business class, was dining on with his ivory chopsticks from a porcelain Ming bowl.

Stars glimmered in the distant night sky. How amazing, one year ago I had almost died. I slept fitfully, woke up in the middle of another kung-fu movie, and thought I heard my lungs rattling, but it was the plane's wings hitting a rough patch. Lightning flashed. *Searching for Confucius* slipped slowly off my knees. I dozed off, woke up to a lovely woman with lush red lips—Julia Roberts speaking flawless Mandarin—and fell back to sleep.

Arriving in Beijing, with puffy eyes and bent backs, we had to catch another two-hour flight into Shantung province, and then we were driven two hours to Qufu. So far, I had seen the interior of two airports and glimpsed distant towns and villages through a van window. Finally, we arrived at the ancient hometown of Confucius and checked into a three-star hotel. I was too excited to sleep. While the rooms and luggage were being sorted out, I stepped outside the lobby into bright daylight.

A wide road extended around the hotel. The sticky air was thick with dust and traffic. Chinese words fluttered from banners on buildings, flashed from sequined billboards and unlit neon signs. My eyes caught sight of tied-down boxes and slatted cages filled with vegetables, flapping chickens and ducks, stacked high on two-wheeled bikes. Squealing pigs cried out from cages piled even higher on wagons pulled along by motorbikes. Engines roared by, sounding as if they were stuck in second gear. Only when all the motorized and man-propelled vehicles came to a halt did I realize that eight roadways intersected within a central paved octagon, with as many angled traffic signals. The signal lights I could see flashed out yellow numbers, counting down to zero, and then the red would turn to green. Before the dust completely settled, the foot traffic would scurry across. A loud beep would sound, the lights would change, and a chaos of wheeled traffic would take over.

I stepped to the edge of the road and gawked like the tourist I was. A truckload of birds and indistinct animals came spinning by, tilting at an impossible angle. I jumped back. The creatures screamed. Feathers of every colour flew into the air. The driver sped up, and momentum rebalanced the tilting load. The bisecting avenues fed into a central roundabout, and every driver navigated by a combination of instinct and luck. One of the bicyclists carrying a towering load of geese nearly spilled sideways. I closed my eyes, imagined blood and guts splattering everywhere. Horns and geese honked. I thought of the recent traffic racing through the arteries of my heart and lungs. When I opened my eyes, the nightmare was gone.

Nothing had spilled.

I spotted a lone figure trapped in the middle of the roundabout. He opened a newspaper and I thought he began reading it, waiting for the light to change. Then I realized that he was making himself appear larger, more significant, like an animal puffing up its fur to make itself fiercer, so that the mad rush of traffic would take notice of him.

The humidity was getting to me. Time to go back into the hotel.

I queried the manager at the desk about the traffic outside. He correctly interpreted my embarrassing fragment of Chinese and my fist slamming into my palm.

"Beep-beep," I said, and made crashing noises.

"Man die two day ago," he said, pointing outside.

Over a cup of tea in the hotel dining room, I wrote in my notebook: *Must survive China.* Pen in hand, I thought of writing a few sentiments of gratitude; instead, I quickly printed, GET A NEWSPAPER!

⁓

Shooting that day was delayed. The promised up-to-date equipment had not been delivered, and three of the crew of six were suspiciously inadequate, except that they were adequately related to the hiring foreman. Explosive exchanges between Trevor and his Chinese counterpart needed to be translated, terms renegotiated. Patrick, the main cameraman and the director of photography, would return to the Chinese television headquarters and make sure the right equipment was selected. The next morning, the English-speaking team met with the Chinese team, tempers simmering, and we departed by car and van with a short, smiling man named Francis—our officially appointed translator—to the first location.

"We're driving to a two-thousand-year-old market square," Carrie, the scriptwriter, told me. "The place dates back to the era of Confucius."

Plenty of ghosts, I thought. My head filled with the historic pageantry of Old China, with a cast of characters dressed in dazzling glitter.

Lines memorized and rehearsed, I stood on the tamped dirt ground, straightened the collar of my black polo shirt, and fussed with the belt loops of my khaki pants. Knees shaky, I moistened my lips, preparing myself to look straight into the camera. No pageantry greeted us, no dazzle, except for the sales banners fluttering from rows of canopied stalls. Torn advertising signs stirred in the warm August breeze. We were milling about in the fabled marketplace, its inhabitants getting ready for the morning's business. Here and there, remnants of walls and broken pillars jutted out of the ground, marking the boundaries of an ancient razed village square.

Families and various independent merchants hurriedly set up their wares. Plain work shirts and pants hung from clotheslines. Hardware, white-and-blue dishes, aluminum pots and iron pans were piled high on counters. Older children stood on stepladders to hang up fist-sized bamboo cages built to house singing crickets, symbols of luck. Livestock farmers lifted up slatted crates stirring with piglets and fowl. Chefs and housewives from the surrounding small towns began their haggling over quality and prices. Eighty years ago, my mother and father, too, must have witnessed such a scene in their home territory of Kwangtung. That air, too, must have smelled of the earthy turnips, heads of cabbage, and butchered meats. But the voices were all foreign to me.

Ready for the first take, I stood in front of a patchwork of bundled herbs, root vegetables, tomatoes, boxes of onions, and layers of gnarled fingers of ginger root. Trevor had pointed out a bright yellow gourd he wanted me to pick up and inspect; then, putting the thing down, I was to turn and greet the sturdy farmer working behind the stall. The old farmer had a dignity about him, and when he was first shown his own face on the portable television monitor, he gave me a proud smile that revealed a broken front tooth. Yes, yes, he wanted to take part. But his eagerness didn't last long: he hadn't expected that our set-up—and Trevor's waiting for just the right slant of sunlight—would eat up over an hour of his market time. His family members, camera shy, stood watching us from a neighbouring stall. His customers stood back to stare at us all standing around. Two women exchanged some words with him; then, to his obvious annoyance, they rushed away with their friends.

Finally, the light was right. Francis again explained to the old man what we were going to do.

The script had required me to comment on this spirit-haunted historic site, while the camera slowly panned from Heaven to Earth, blue sky to ground.

"The disciples of Confucius," I began, "must have once wandered through this same marketplace . . ."

In a two-shot close-up, I asked the old man what the legendary Confucius had meant to him. While the camera focused on the wrinkled, sunburnt face, Francis translated my brief question.

With barely a pause, back came the old farmer's animated answer, his village sibilants hissing out of the broken-toothed mouth. He waved a callused hand over the vegetables, seemed to make some comments about the gourd I had admired, and ended by pointing a finger at the cabbages and the basket of turnips. I wondered what the root vegetables had to do with Confucius. I waited for Francis's translation.

After scribbling some notes he had jotted down on a small pad, Francis came out with a stream of formal English, every word praising Master Confucius. Curiously, his translation lasted many times longer than the original response. He stopped. I waited for any mention of cabbages or turnips. Or perfect gourds. There was none.

I asked a second brief question.

Back came an even briefer answer from the stall seller, this time accompanied by a grunt.

Francis dutifully finished making some notes and began to "translate" the man's answer, sans grunt: "For thousands of years, we the people have revered the great Confucius . . ." and so on, and so on.

The old man we left behind in the stall looked dismayed. I had no language to apologize for our abrupt departure. I felt guilty, as if we had set him up simply to be exploited and dismissed without a second thought.

Now I was to wander between the aisles of canopied stands, stopping here and there, a diaspora son visiting the open marketplace of his ancestors. A few old people held moon-faced children wriggling on their laps, while the young parents busied themselves with packaging goods and haggling. Chickens, ducks, and fattened geese cackled in their cages. Behind them, boiling pots of water stood waiting to loosen their feathers. I thought of Vancouver's Market Street, smelled again the slaughter of birds trailing ribbons of blood from their sliced throats, thrashing away their last moments in deep wooden barrels that resounded like drums.

"Action," Trevor said.

Before each take, someone brusquely cleared curious onlookers out of the camera's range. The Chinese crew of six took up their stations; one waited for instructions and then fumbled with the extension cords. Metres of electrical cords, recording devices, lighting equipment, generators, and a television monitor trailed behind me. And I was to walk and talk as if the motley crew were not there.

I could not get the old man out of my mind: I wanted to go back and tell him how he reminded me of the bachelor elders of Chinatown, those men who were abandoned by the railroad contractors, dismissed without a second thought, their peasant words meaningless to their white bosses. Once, I had witnessed my father speak his broken English without effect to a drunk who confronted him in our restaurant and then stormed out cursing *shit-ass goddamned Chinks.* The old farmer had the same look of despair my father had had when he turned to look at my mother and me, as if suddenly he could not breathe the same air, for the air and the place, even his family, seemed no longer to belong to him.

That whole day's travel, with relocations, set-ups, and filming, plus a lunch break, lasted seven hours. The panned shots of my strolling down the aisles of this ancient market site were eventually mixed with footage of me walking among the outdoor stalls of Vancouver's Chinatown—a symbolic eclipse of two thousand years of shopping-as-usual. The sequence lasted no more than a few blinks of an eye. Between blinks, I thought of that man flapping open the newspaper in the mad rush of Qufu traffic to make himself larger, more significant; I wished I had made myself bigger to that farmer. I wished I had paused to flap open my wallet, and bought from him that yellow gourd. In the end, his part would lie coiled on the cutting-room floor.

On the eighth day, during a long break waiting for our third new translator to arrive (Francis had been given some days off), Patrick and I wandered through the massive parklands dedicated to Confucius and his heirs. We explored the ancient site of the Family Mansion, the residence of Confucius's descendants, built next to the Confucian Temple. No one was there. We stood in the doorway of one of the rooms and stared down an empty hall stretching away from us like a tunnel a city block long, the wall covered with Chinese script. Our voices echoed against the high complex of ceilings.

Here, in framed rectangles along the wall, glued or nailed halfway from the ceiling down to its bottom ledge, are the names of more than eighty generations who were given the imperial privilege to be interred in these acres of historic burial plots, their direct Confucian lineage documented on bamboo slats, carved on stone and wood tablets. Standing in this ancient hall of the Kong Family Mansion, I thought, in awe, that I should at last feel *something* about being here in China. As a child, the Chinatown elders had shouted at me, *You skin yellow! You proud*

Chinese! You always be Chinese! Here, everything surrounding me was Chinese. Yet I felt no pride, and I did not feel *Chinese.*

What was I resisting?

I lifted a finger and gently touched one of the memorial plaques. How *foreign* everything felt.

"Can you read any of these names?" Patrick asked me.

"No," I said. I could read the Chinese numbers, perhaps even roughly figure out some of the dates. That was all. "You and Carrie know more Chinese than I do."

The two had learned to speak Mandarin for their film work in Asia, enough to win the respect of the local crew. Carrie, in fact, had grown up in China and was able to converse with Francis. Patrick caught my moment of isolation.

"Don't forget," he said cheerfully, "you're still more connected to all of this than Carrie and I could ever be."

Not true, I thought. I shrugged.

Patrick would not relent. "Doesn't this place do something to you?"

There was only one day left of filming. In the beginning, I had felt the excitement of working on a film, a jolt now and again of pleasure before the camera's eye. But now I was beginning to feel like a fraud. My confidence drained away.

"All those great sayings of Confucius"—Patrick's voice was upbeat—"Wayson, you know so many of them!"

I did know them, but I had been repressing my desire to understand *something else:* Wasn't I, by blood, Chinese? Hadn't I come here to discover how much of my life and my writings were connected to Confucian philosophies? I secretly longed to belong to this historical place in some vivid, romantic way. *Only connect*, E. M. Forster had written. I had been properly awed by the relics and respectful of the carved names. But I had felt that same pride before the castles of Europe, before the Acropolis, not because I was English or French or German or Greek but because I was a human being and belonged to a race of creatures capable of making so much beauty and extravagance.

Here I felt no deep or serious connection to anything. I began to choke. Dust motes danced in the rays of light coming through cracks in the walls. My chest tightened. I took out my puffer and inhaled. As my lungs expanded, I surrendered any idea that I had ever walked these halls in splendid silk robes.

"Wayson, isn't there anything you really want from this trip?"

Patrick's question came to me like a bolt of lightning. I swallowed hard. I felt something relentless and true, a kind of exploding freedom. I couldn't help it. I started to laugh, and my laughter echoed down the dimly lit hall of the Family Mansion.

"What's so funny?"

"Confucius say," I said, "'I'm such a banana!' Do you know what I really want, Patrick?"

"What?"

"A fortune cookie."

The last hours of shooting took place early the next morning at the grave of Confucius. Here I was to tell the story of his death at age seventy-three, of the sad circumstances in which he had outlived his only son and his wife. How shortly after their loss, he had heard of the death of his favourite student. How he met his end believing he had utterly failed: the warring princes and dukes of his time continuing their destructive, killing ways.

I stood before the solitary stone hut, built in honour of Zi Gong, one of his last students, who, mourning the loss of the Master, did not leave the gravesite for six years. Zi Gong's loyal gesture assured that others came to know of Confucius. The Master's wandering disciples who came back to visit the grave would forever commemorate the site.

Confucius died broken-hearted, unaware that his fame as a teacher, his inspiring attempts to civilize a savage world, would remain relevant for all humanity. I thought of my father, who used to recite the classic sayings and who told me mythic stories about this wise teacher. Of course, I had listened to none of it, yet somehow a legacy was left to me through two thousand years of history, down through the words of my father that flew past my know-it-all ears, and finally through the civilized ways in which my mother and father and the community of Vancouver's Chinatown had nurtured my in-between generation. I felt renewed. An unbroken chain of human intention had at last become a part of me.

In Beijing, faithful Elaine waited for me at the airport. Our plan had been to spend two days together in the capital city, but the filming in Qufu had gone overtime, and now I could only wait six hours at the Beijing airport for my scheduled flight back to Canada. Elaine waited with me.

"How was your first time in China?" she asked. "How was Qufu?"

I couldn't quite tell her. But pushing through the alien crowds to make my way back home, I knew now, with certainty, where my bones belonged.

Chapter 13

⁓

THE CHINA TRIP HAD INFLAMED MY DESIRE TO LIVE MY life as usual—to keep busy, to be useful and feel truly needed. I had been lucky in China: there had been no heat inversions, no medical problems. I had escaped using my puffer too often, and never even unpacked my surgical masks. I was not afraid of dying. Hadn't I already been there and bought the T-shirt? I rushed back to living my life.

I gave my three writing classes twice the required number of assignments. I visited book clubs and rarely turned down charity events, and accepted many dinner invitations. I wrote and rewrote my manuscript pages, sometimes until four in the morning. I promised myself a trip to Vancouver for some fresh research.

By the end of that semester, I was feeling the effects of having deprived myself of sleep. In a futile effort to catch up, I slept until eleven on the weekends and woke up groggy, the taste of mint mouthwash on my tongue, grumbling at having slept away the morning. My head was buzzing with ideas and the insights

I had garnered about myself in China. I was excited at the possibility that my second novel would be rewritten at a deeper level. The themes of bones and belonging and family, and of being a neither-this-nor-that, had been incubating long enough.

Those booklets from the Heart and Stroke Foundation, those pamphlets and diet sheets I took away from Riverdale and St. Mike's—after a quick reading, I piled all of them into a file I marked VERY IMPORTANT.

My honest intention to keep in good physical health didn't last long. The brisk daily walks—*boring!*—were the first to go. The days were getting too cold. The ice too treacherous. The chill in the air bad for my asthma. Scheduled indoor exercises degenerated into my falling asleep on my trendy yoga mat; or leaning my head against the refrigerator door, wondering what to snack on next; or throwing my growing weight against the frozen car door. Three times I did attempt to shovel my tires out of a deep snowfall, but each time Karl stopped me.

"Watch your heart," he said, taking the shovel from me and finishing the job.

That same fall I had been diagnosed as a borderline Type 2 diabetic. But from eating well and wisely—mixed greens, beans, skinless chicken, no sugary desserts—I soon returned to eating five times more of everything I craved, leaving most of the greens behind. In the solemn belief that I was burning the midnight oil, and not getting enough fuel into my body, I ate plenty of chops, steaks, and comforting bowls of pastas and Chinese savouries at dim sum brunches to get more energy. My thirty-six-inch-plus pants fitted me fine. And if ever I wanted to look slimmer, extra-large tops came in handy. When I checked myself in the mirror, I admired how the abundant shirt material vanquished the blimp-like belly; how the love handles poked out like high-rise hips.

My joints began to creak and my limbs moved as if weighted sacks held me down. By the end of the third winter, I could barely walk up to my third-floor classroom without gasping for five minutes. At home, climbing the stairs to my attic space, I secretly paused between flights to catch my breath. My body demanded attention, my brain refused to grant it.

Between uses of my puffers—I resorted to them for some relief—a vision began to haunt me. I remembered when I was five, Mother holding tightly on to my hand to keep me back from a group of white-haired men working through a traditional pattern of tai chi exercises. We were standing on the gravel rooftop patio at Kam Yen Jan, the Chinese sausage factory where Mother worked during the war years. The old men, numbering five—I counted them on my fingers—shifted their hands and lifted their feet as if in a slow-motion dream. At the sound of a clapper, one man called out a step, "Standing crane," and the five transformed into cranes with wings outspread while balanced on one leg, exactly like the birds I had seen on painted scrolls. "Curving snake," another called out, and tense, lithe bodies twisted soundlessly into serpents sliding against the sky. "Crouching tiger," came the next command, and soon gnarled fingers were bent like tiger paws posed to strike. The pleasure of this memory came back again and again to me, increasing with such intensity that it was a sign I could not ignore.

When I asked the Humber College nurse for advice, she told me to sign up with a personal trainer. She gave me some names. Not one of the three I interviewed seemed too keen to take me on, especially after testing my fitness and hearing about my recent medical traumas. After I nearly completed ten push-ups, one even shook his watch to see if my heart was actually beating that rapidly. The most idealistic trainer lasted four sessions with me. Karl and Marie refused to let me fall back into my cheerful denial.

"I'm fine," I would say, pushing aside the salad Marie had served me. "Look at me. I've been working as hard as ever and I feel—"

"You look like shit," Karl said.

I climbed up to my room, barely able to make it to the mirror. I took a hard look at myself. My face was ashen from the effort. My wheezing was audible, threatening. That December day, in the dean's office, I signed the papers that ended a forty-year career.

My friend Kathleen suggested that I work with her husband, a marathon runner who had recently been certified as a personal trainer.

Mohammad Hessian did not look like a serious runner, at least not the tall, lanky type I had in mind. He had the face of a Persian prince; his tight, compact body stood a bit shorter than my bulging, convex one. He smiled so warmly, with such masculine confidence, that I could understand how Kathleen had fallen so hard. If he minded the privilege I took of calling him by Kathleen's affectionate name—Rami—he never let on. His eyes gleamed with intelligence.

"Don't worry," he said, "I'll for sure give you a call in January." With a slight and elegant bow, he urged me to taste some Iranian savouries he had baked for a party.

Kathleen saw my look of surprise and broke into cascading laughter.

"Yes, Wayson," she said, catching my breath for me. "He cooks, too."

"I've had a heart attack," I said at once when Rami and I got together for the first evaluation. "I can't do much. I think my other trainers got bored—or maybe all three were scared they'd lose their licence if I died on them." Rami raised a brow at that, as if he were sensing a challenge. "One trainer tested me and shouted out that I just got a perfect score out of ten—a *zero*."

"Well," Rami said, "not many people score perfect."

We both laughed. He took a long pause to emphasize that his next statement was to be taken seriously. "I never mind being bored."

He told me that as a boy he had survived the Iran-Iraq war. For him, boring was good.

From the first stretching exercises he assigned me in my living room—and which he heartily demonstrated on his mat—to a later schedule of lifting weights, Rami had a knack for sensing how far I could go and had fascinating methods for distracting me from the effort.

"Oh, they have such ways to tell you about love," he would say of Iranian poets as he held my wrist higher into the air, then pushed my shoulder back. "They make me think of Iran, the time before music was banned."

For our forty-five-minute walks on the less bitter days, Rami drove me to Taylor Creek, where he caught me by the arm if I tripped over a branch or skidded on a sheet of ice hidden beneath dead leaves. As winter withdrew, we began a light jog along the creaking boardwalk in the Beach under budding oaks and willows, and along streets lined with rows of maples. His eyes scanned ahead to direct us away from loose boards or around broken pieces of sidewalk.

"Isn't the air great?" he would say, and I would follow suit and take as deep a breath as I dared.

On these walks and jogs, Rami's many stories about his adolescence in Iran kept me from being bored. I shared my personal stories, too; they interested him perhaps because they were free of the savagery, the still unspeakable details, that would wake him up in a sweat. He smiled at my good fortune, appreciated the plight of the Chinatown immigrants who'd had family left behind in China when Japan invaded. At the shocking news of their sons and daughters dying, the immigrants would wail in the kin-named tong halls of Chinatown, where their loss was posted in words brushed in black calligraphy on strips of white ribbon. I was only six when the war ended; I barely remember much else, but I recall the screams and cries and how Mother held her palms tightly against my ears.

"Certain sounds you never forget," Rami said, and he clenched his fists.

In wartorn Iran, he'd experienced his own brand of luck. At sixteen, Rami had a third of his lungs removed because of potentially malignant cysts. When he turned seventeen—his heart filled with patriotic fervour to fight the enemies of Iran— he boldly volunteered to complete his mandatory two-year military service. Noticing the deep scar running along his rib cage, the army rejected him. Only boys and men with a healthy set of lungs were permitted to face cannon fire.

He could not serve his country, nor could he stay at home and do nothing but dodge bullets and bombs while his friends were being slaughtered. He journeyed by foot through Turkey and Greece, found a way to Germany to earn a living in a factory, and finally found one more adventure on a freighter to Japan and another factory job. From there, with a survivor's vocabulary of six languages in his head, he applied to come to Canada.

As he talked, plainly and carefully, of the past, he reminded me of those "no surrender" Chinatown pioneers who helped to raise me.

"I went through many difficulties," he would say, as a simple statement of fact. "So lucky to be here now."

"Me, too," I said, and we both laughed.

⁓

A week before I was to leave for a visit to Vancouver, we stood on the sandy shore along the boardwalk, stood together to observe someone paragliding, his body hanging in the air as the motorboat towing him roared by, propelling the huge sail to drift about like a wayward parachute. We sat down on a boulder on the beach and watched the man splash down and swim safely back to shore. His friends ran to greet him. Something—perhaps the distant roar and sudden whine of the boat engine gearing down, then the abrupt silence—reminded Rami of a rocket or a bomb spinning down from the sky.

"I know that I was lucky, Wayson, for sure, but many of my friends didn't make it. Many came back broken, you know, missing arms and legs. Blind and deaf. Crazy. In my nightmares, it's me that has gone crazy. I feel guilty. No one wins."

"But, Rami, you have to know you're saving my life," I said.

"No, no," he said, vigorously shaking his head. "You save your own life. I don't think you want to die."

"No," I said, and meant to add *Not at all* when my heart began to race and I was back in the intensive care unit, my lungs tightening, throat muscles cramping up, choking me. I shoved my hand into my pocket, grabbed for the puffer, and inhaled two blasts. Rami stood and watched, trying not to add to my misery: he recognized the panic that for a few seconds would paralyze my speech. It had happened twice before. He recognized what was happening to me, knew I was experiencing a flashback. Tosh had warned me about them, the harsh, jolting recalls, relentlessly real, that would leave me frustrated and angry. I could still evoke the Queen of Water sneering at my thirst, the slobbering dog licking at my wrist.

"Never, ever, going to be sick like that again," I said.

"You promise me, Wayson?"

As I extended my hand to shake on it, Rami grabbed at me and gave me what must have been an Iranian wrestler's hug, nearly knocking me over. We half turned, then turned again— and finally his arm reached around me to stop me from falling.

"That was great," I said, as he hauled me back to my feet. "I could die happy now."

Chapter 14

"STAY AS LONG AS YOU NEED TO," ALICE SAID. "WE'VE
missed you! Vancouver missed you!"

Settled in at Jake and Alice's comfortable downstairs suite, I
felt at home. I had known them since my early university days
in 1959, when I took Jake's short-story class. During the first
few classes, I thought Jake too mild mannered to be taken seriously. He approached his classes like a boxer stepping aside to
expose the students who might like to challenge him. He
approached his opponents with measured caution before deter-
mining exactly the right second to strike. By the fourth class,
few would mistake Jake's quiet, deliberate ways for signs of
weakness. The man taught me how to write.

Jake's wife, Alice, suited him beautifully. From the first time
I was introduced to her at an English Department party, she
looked royal to me.

This visit to Vancouver, four months after I had retired from
Humber, marked four decades of Jake and Alice's sheltering
generosity towards me. Over the past ten years, the carpeted,

furnished basement suite had come to feel like my own place—a large room with a double bed and a sprawling desk I could instantly clutter with books and papers.

I had come out west to do more writing and to arrange for some interviews. The unfinished novel, now two years delayed, was becoming unmanageable. Jake and Alice were two I counted on to review the manuscript. Alice often caught hairline flaws that others would miss.

"I acted out your description on page 200," she noted. "I don't think Jenny can bend that way unless she's a contortionist."

I informed Alice that I was heading out for a quick lunch and some rethinking of that whole scene. I needed to un-pretzel Jenny.

That Sunday, when I stepped into the Mekong Restaurant at their busiest time, I caught the vigilant hostess by surprise. For a few seconds, the petite Vietnamese woman stood immovable.

When I had been in Vancouver the year before I had missed Victoria. I looked around. The walls decorated by a former Greek owner, with trailing vines and faded island vistas and impossibly blue skies, had not changed. I took a deep breath. Maybe my hands shook a little too obviously. I blamed the jet lag. My ears still felt a little plugged, my muscle coordination remained a little off, and my face looked much thinner than the last time Victoria had seen me, now two years ago; the hair, thinner, too. I had visibly aged.

Victoria didn't immediately flash her welcoming smile. Instead, she looked to the right and left of me. Customers were making their way towards the last empty tables. She came forward, let out a sigh, and smiled.

"You look lovely as ever," I said.

She did. She kept staring at me.

I laughed. "Do I look okay to you?"

Too abruptly, she said, "Oh yes, yes, Mr. Wayson." Finally, the warmth returned to her eyes. "We so busy now."

She picked up some cups and a pot of tea from the table beside her and pointed towards the sunlit row of French windows where some customers sat waiting. "I go there now, Mr. Wayson," she said. "Cousin Tam take care of you."

Cousin Tam guided me to the last empty table of the long room and handed me a menu. Before I could focus on the list of Thai and Vietnamese specials, Tam asked if a young couple might share the table. I didn't mind at all.

It felt good to be at Victoria's place again, even sitting at a table smack in the middle of the room, instead of the very last table at the back I usually occupied near the kitchen entrance. Over the course of four years of interviews for my novel, conducted during my spring and summer breaks, that back table had been my makeshift desk, where I treated elders and friends to late lunches in exchange for their vivid memories of Chinatown and, with luck, a rare secret.

I poured myself some light jasmine. I caught Victoria glancing at me from across the dining room. She looked concerned.

Halfway through my lunch, a mixed plate of noodles, stir-fry veggies, and lemongrass chicken, Victoria came to the table and gently touched my hand. She made small talk about the nice sunshine that I must have brought with me from Toronto, and tipped back the lid of the teapot to signal for another pot. The cook shouted from the kitchen, and she excused herself. Customers were lined up at the entrance, but still Cousin Tam brought me over a fresh pot of tea and a clean cup.

"Victoria say you like this kind better," he said, pouring a cup for me. "Good for the blood."

The couple sharing my table paused over their luncheon specials. I pretended not to notice. I sipped from my cup of fresh good-for-the-blood tea and savoured the bitter aroma. Unlike the light jasmine, this tea had no hints of perfumed blossoms; rather, the taste of bark and strong herbs reminded me of the black tea Mother and Father brewed for each other to strengthen themselves during the long afternoons of their final years.

I finished my meal, swallowed one more mouthful of the dark tea, and paid my bill. I waved goodbye to Victoria through the kitchen transom. She ran up to the pass-through counter, wiping her hands on some paper towels.

"Come back soon," she said. "Next time I say proper hello and talk to you."

I nodded happily.

She extended her hand for me to shake. She held on for a second longer and said, "Great importance to talk."

"Something wrong?"

"Oh no, no—just for talk. Like we do every time you come."

"I'm here for a few weeks," I rushed to explain. "I'll be back for a late lunch tomorrow with my friend Larry."

"Yes, yes," she said. "Bring Larry. Be sure come back."

When I entered the Mekong the next day, Larry, from the Vancouver Chinatown Museum, sat waiting for me at one of the side tables. At two-thirty, the place was empty. I could see that Victoria was in the kitchen helping to clean up the lunchtime dishes. She looked through the transom and waved.

"You're early," I said to Larry.

"You're late," he said, laughing a little nervously. "Victoria insisted you were here before me."

"Not really. I walked by twenty minutes ago and didn't see you, so I went to pick up some coffee beans. Anyway, she must have seen me go past."

"Not really," Larry said. He looked anxiously around the restaurant. "See those wind chimes at the back of the room?"

A drooping wind chime hung against the wall by the kitchen door.

"What about them?"

Larry looked knowingly at me and lowered his voice. "You better ask Victoria."

I didn't entirely appreciate his reticence. I had a dozen questions to ask him about some elders, veterans of the Second World War, details I needed for a scene. I pulled out a notebook from my briefcase, ready to get down to business. Suddenly, Victoria stood by the table. She put down the menus and set the table with napkins, a teapot, and teacups.

"Mr. Wayson," she began, "last day you were here at my restaurant there were two others with you."

"No," I protested. "I was by myself. That young couple joined me because there was no place else for them."

"Yes, I know that," she said. She poured tea into the cups.

Jasmine perfumed the air. "But just the same, two others with you."

I shook my head. She repeated herself, and this time she looked at Larry, who answered her knowing glance with a conspiratorial nod.

"Only me," I said. "I came in by myself."

"No, no, two others with you."

Victoria stiffened her back. I followed her eyes and together we stared at Larry. Larry was only three months older than me, but he had been raised in the very heart of Pender and Main, so I figured he was more sensitive to Old Chinatown ways. Victoria had been born in Vietnam to immigrants who had come from a village in Old China.

Exasperated by their air of mystery, I blurted out, "Do you mean two ghosts walked in with me?"

"Yes," came their reply.

Victoria put one hand on the table and bent low to my ear. In a stage whisper she said, "*They still here.*"

I saw nothing. Nothing but empty air. What had happened to my friend? Victoria and I had a cozy, above-board relationship. We traded the usual everyday greetings, a few words about Vancouver restaurant life, how her children were doing, how my books were written. Never once had she looked at me as she was now doing, eyebrows raised, mesmerized by the empty air around me. She lifted her hand off the table and delicately pointed behind me.

"Right there," she said. "Next to your chair."

No one was there, but that didn't discourage Larry from his intense focus or stop Victoria from talking.

"The two have to go," she said. "They can't stay with you, Mr. Wayson Choy."

Surprised to hear her use my full name so assertively, I worried about our relationship. Hadn't I long ago encouraged her to call me Wayson? She couldn't, she told me, because I was "a fine gentleman, a professor and a writer." We compromised with Mr. Wayson.

"Well, Victoria, they're not bothering me. I don't feel threatened."

I didn't want to encourage the drama, but I couldn't resist: "I trust the two are good spirits."

"Oh yes," she said and broke into a broad smile. "The two love you very much. They don't want to leave you. The old woman feel very guilty. She never again want to leave you."

"Well," I said, at a loss for something to say, "that's nice." Larry frowned. I couldn't blame him. I too bristled at my condescending tone. "I'm fine with all this, Victoria. If the two spirits don't mean me any harm, maybe Larry and I could look at the list of specials?"

Victoria put her hand over the menus. "Mr. Wayson," she said. "May I ask your permission to speak about this to my friend?" Victoria anticipated my question. "My friend Artemis. She know so much, very sensitive person. May I ask her about all this?"

I decided the best thing to do was to submit and get it over with. "Yes, of course," I said. "You have my permission to talk to Artemis if you think it'll help. Now, Larry, what about the lemongrass chicken and noodles?"

But Larry was hooked. He asked Victoria if she could see

my two companions clearly enough to describe them. To my annoyance, she nodded.

"One is old woman, she the one feeling very guilty about leaving Mr. Wayson the last time. The other one is a young boy, maybe a very young man, who never say goodbye to him. He love him, too." She turned back to me, eyes watering. "They don't want to leave you. They don't want to hurt you, Mr. Wayson."

I bit. "Why do they have to leave me at all if, as you say, they don't want to hurt me?"

Victoria shook her head at how little I understood. "Oh, Mr. Wayson, they must leave you or you get in trouble. I ask my friend Artemis."

"Yes, of course, and I'll have the lemongrass chicken," I said. "And Larry?"

I kicked him under the table. He ordered.

Victoria went away to the kitchen.

"Larry, what were you two talking about before I came in?"

"Sonny," he said, using a name that dated back to our kindergarten days together, "she told me about that wind chime at the back. She says that they took it away from the front windows because it made too much noise, but ever since, she has noticed that whenever a certain someone is going to come into the restaurant, it shakes."

"Someone? Who?"

"Just you. She told the kitchen help yesterday morning that Mr. Wayson would be showing up. And you did. It's happened before."

I sighed. A mere coincidence. "And these two so-called ghosts?"

"Sonny, they're the hungry ghosts that the elders used to warn us about. Those spirits who are always looking for a way back into life. They're dangerous because they use up your life energy to stay with you. My father and your Third Uncle used to talk about them."

"You don't really believe in all this stuff, do you?"

Larry shrugged. "Who knows? My father used to say that people sometimes want their loved ones back, even as hungry ghosts."

Clearly Larry was more Chinatown than Sonny Choy could ever be. Our meals arrived.

"Eat," I said, my response to most awkward situations. Larry picked up his chopsticks. I started on my bowl of won tons. Nothing more was said about ghosts, hungry or otherwise.

By the end of our almost two-hour lunch, everything had returned to normal. Before we parted, Larry and I arranged to meet again later in the week.

When I stepped through the front door and saw Jake and Alice working together on the *Sun* crossword in the living room, I decided to say nothing about my afternoon at the Mekong. What was there to say? In the community that raised me, I overheard constant talk of ghost sightings, even witnessed a few elders talking at them. But I never saw a single one. And I saw nothing at the Mekong. Ghosts were everywhere, but I did not believe in them.

That Friday, Larry and I met again at the Mekong. Victoria took our orders in a businesslike fashion. She served our lunches, poured us tea, and went back to the kitchen.

I ate, drank cups of tea, and made notes from what Larry told me he had uncovered at the archives about Chinese Canadians who fought as soldier-spies for the Allies. These adventurous young men volunteered for the tough training in guerrilla tactics. They studied Japanese in a secret camp near Penticton, B.C.; then they were shipped to Australia and India for field training before being deployed in the jungles of Malaysia, Burma, Sumatra, and Borneo. With their immersion in the language and ways of the Japanese, and with their Asian faces, these Chinatown sons could penetrate the enemy lines better than any Caucasian.

"The government finally gave the Chinese something important to do," I said.

Larry laughed. "The dirty stuff, of course."

When the dishes were cleared, I spread the photocopies of military documents and news clippings that my friend had found for me. Midway through one set of papers, we paused as if we had finished our work. Victoria approached the table.

"I spoke with Artemis," she said.

Before I could stop him, Larry said, "What did she say about the ghosts?"

"They have to leave Mr. Wayson," she looked at me. "Artemis said that you will go somewhere, a place far away from here, this fall, maybe over the ocean?" I refused to confirm or deny the query. Then she dropped the bombshell. "For sure, you travel far away. You must tell the ghosts to leave you, Mr. Wayson. Tell them to go back. Artemis say that if the ghosts do not go away, you will come back home in a . . . a . . . wh-wheelchair." The sudden rising pitch in her voice made me wonder what she had actually intended to say.

"Are you sure you mean a wheelchair?"

"Yes, yes," Victoria said as she recovered her composure. "A wh-wheelchair. Do you plan to go over the ocean, Mr. Wayson?"

I could not think of anyone in Vancouver who would know of the invitation I had received to attend a ten-day creative writing program at the University of Siena that fall. I had been asked to keep the invitation under my hat, and the details for the trip were still far from confirmed.

"You go over the ocean, Mr. Wayson?"

"I don't think so," I answered. "But if I happened to go overseas . . . ?"

"You come back in wheelchair," Victoria repeated, too matter-of-factly, I thought. "That's what Artemis want to warn you. If ghosts don't leave you, you come back in a wheelchair."

I bit my lip, tried to resist, but couldn't. "What else did Artemis say?"

"I ask her about going to our temple for a ritual. Maybe ask the Buddhist monk to help tell the ghosts to leave."

"An exorcism?"

"Yes, the priest and the temple people use a kind of special prayer. Help you tell them to go back. Do you know the old woman spirit? She feel so bad to leave you. Very guilty. She don't want to leave you again."

Larry stared at me. Eight years ago, at fifty-six, I had discovered I was adopted. Could the ghost with me now be my biological mother? Victoria went on to describe the young man—his high forehead, sad eyes set wide apart. I couldn't help myself: I thought at once of Philip.

"Very sad eyes. He miss you," she concluded, "and very good looking. You must let him go."

Philip was nineteen when I was seventeen, and we shared a strong emotional relationship. When my mother and I moved back for the second time to the town of Belleville, Ontario, to work in the new fish-and-chip restaurant my father had bought, Philip wrote me letters that I intended to answer. But I couldn't find the words to write about my feelings for him, feelings that frightened me. Then one afternoon our mutual friend Bill phoned me from Vancouver to say that Philip had died of leukemia. He died without ever hearing from me. We never had a chance to say goodbye.

"Very handsome young man," Victoria said. "Have very strong feelings for you."

Two ghosts from my past? Ghosts of possibilities? No, I concluded. Coincidences! Nothing more.

No doubt Artemis had entrapped poor superstitious Victoria into a scheme to extract money from me, the undoubtedly wealthy bestselling writer. Then the joke would be on them.

"Can I speak to Artemis myself?"

Without hesitation, Victoria said, "Yes. I write you her phone number."

I suspected I would call, get an appointment, and only then be informed of her hourly fee. Would it be fifty bucks? Seventy-five? One hundred dollars?

I paid the lunch bill and took the piece of paper handed to me.

"You're really going to call her?" Larry asked.

"You bet I am," I said.

⟿

"May I speak to Artemis, please?"

"Yes," said a plain voice. "Speaking."

"This is Victoria's friend Wayson Choy—"

"Oh yes, her writer friend." The woman's voice remained calm. "I hope I've been helpful."

"Well, yes," I said. "I'm calling to make a specific appointment with you and, of course, I'll pay you your full fee." I emphasized *full fee*. Someone had to rescue poor Victoria from whatever scam she was caught up in. "I'm only here for a week and if you could just see me—"

"No, not possible," came the answer, so quickly that it took me off guard. "I'm very busy these days. Please understand. I'm working with cancer patients, and I'm just too exhausted to take on new clients. If you'd like to ask anything, just let Victoria know."

"She won't see me," I told Alice and Jake, who were in on my plan to bust the scam. "She works with cancer patients. Too tired. Not only will this Artemis not see me," I continued, "she didn't ask for a single penny from me."

Jake tried to make me feel more confident about my junior-detective instincts. He leaned over the kitchen table, thought a moment, and I saw him young again, his voice comforting.

"I bet when you have that Buddhist ritual, Wayson, they'll ask for some donation . . . I'm sure of it."

⁓

A few mornings later, I met Victoria at the back of the restaurant and she drove to the Buddhist Temple on First Avenue. I was to leave for Toronto in less than a week, so arrangements for the exorcism, the particular ritual that would encourage the two spirits to leave me and return to the Other Side, needed to be put in place. First, I had to go to the temple and answer some questions. Victoria was with me to translate.

It was a cool, bright spring morning. Doubts had crept into my head about the situation. An exorcism? What could that be like? I could only think of the ones I had seen in horror movies like *The Exorcist.* I couldn't shake off my doubts about Victoria's seeing those two ghosts, nor could I let go of the curiosity that made me want to go through with everything . . . *just in case.*

I walked up to the high bars of the wrought-iron gate. Between the bars, and hanging on a wooden door a few feet away, a framed sign in English and Vietnamese read, in barely legible letters, Sorry Closed. Beneath those words, the hours were listed: Open Today at Noon to . . .

I stopped Victoria and pointed to the sign. She squinted to decipher the smaller Vietnamese words.

"No, no, can't be!" she protested. "I must open restaurant at eleven."

"Gate's locked," I said.

Victoria yanked at the bars like a frantic prisoner and gripped the handle. With a distinct click, the high gate swung open.

Victoria stepped over the threshold and walked the few steps towards the wooden door. She turned the handle and boldly strode in. I closed the gate behind me and followed her into the hall. Lots of polished beams and shining floors.

"I know we to be here today," Victoria insisted. "I know."

The vast hall was bright with morning light. On one side of us was a glassed-in bulletin board with announcements written in Vietnamese and scattered English phrases; there were posters, pictures of children, some in baseball uniforms. On the opposite side, an entranceway revealed a corridor that led to a staircase; farther down the hall was an archway through which I could see three big Buddhas. I recognized the middle Buddha, the largest one, legs crossed, in eternal meditation. Potted leafy green plants sat at the base. The sun poured through banks of leaded-glass windows, the light falling in a crisscross pattern. Rows and rows of carved tables and chairs were set up for ceremonial purposes. The air smelled of sandalwood and polish and made my throat itch. I felt for my inhaler, but I had forgotten to bring it.

"No one's here," I said. Against Victoria's sincere faith in these matters, my unsettled doubts began to make me feel a little queasy, a bit of a fraud. "We should go."

"No, no, Mr. Wayson. I call for someone."

Victoria ducked into the small entrance and boldly hollered out something in Vietnamese. Her speech echoed. Someone bustled. An elderly woman, hair in a bun, gripping her kimono and tying a final knot, came rushing towards us. Sharp-sounding words were exchanged. Victoria seemed to be getting nowhere.

"She ask how possible we are in here," Victoria translated. "She says not possible we are in here. Gate locked. I told her you have to be here, Mr. Wayson."

Since we refused to leave, the old lady pushed us aside, opened the wooden door, shook out a chain of keys from a side pocket, and stepped out to lock the iron gate.

"Tell her I'm here for an exorcism," I said. "Tell her something. Tell her it's urgent. She's probably going to call the police on us."

The old woman stepped back in, swinging her keys. Victoria spoke louder. The old woman heard her out, then she turned her thin head towards me; her narrow eyes looked me up and down. Neither woman spoke. Finally, the old woman said a few words and disappeared into the corridor. Her sandalled feet whispered up the staircase.

"What's happening?"

"The Master is not in. The lady going to wake up his student to interview you."

"You told her about—?"

"Yes, she understand right away."

"I mean," I said, "what about the gate? Did she understand it was unlocked?"

"She said no way that gate be open."

The old woman had claimed she had locked it herself after the previous night's ceremonies. At the mention of the exorcism ritual, however, she had calmed down immediately.

"The woman say the gate unlock by itself for you, Mr. Wayson." Victoria gave me a beatific smile. "Just for you."

A sign.

I stiffened. I fought against the irrational urge to believe her. What was there to debate? The gate couldn't have just unlocked itself, but I thought it best not to state the obvious fact that a forgetful old woman's lapse had allowed a squeaky handle to turn, a rusty lock to click, and two innocents to trespass.

"I go pray for you," Victoria told me. She approached the main altar and lit three sticks of incense, grateful that the spirits attending me were loving ones. She bowed three times and serenely petitioned Buddha to guide them back to the Other Side. Her dark hair shone in the sun.

My lungs felt a bit tight. I walked away from the main room and back down the hallway. The smell of worship, of incense, permeated the place. I began to wheeze. I leaned against the wooden door. I heard the iron gate rattle. Someone was shaking it. The handle began to squeal. How could I have forgotten my puffer? I held my breath. After a few seconds, the silence returned. Whoever wanted in had turned away.

⌁

The sound of muffled feet from the corridor, followed by heavier footsteps, alerted me. I raised my head from the door and called to Victoria.

"They're coming down the stairs," I said.

The old woman stepped out of the corridor and bowed to the young man behind her. Victoria greeted him in Vietnamese and explained our purpose for being there. The old woman excused herself from our company.

I took a good look at the Master's acolyte. His clear eyes, high forehead, perfect mouth—and his composure—took me aback. I thought of Housman's "To an Athlete Dying Young." I thought of Philip. As he led us so confidently into the room of the three deities to sit across from him at one of the tables, I had to pinch myself. As he and Victoria carried on in Vietnamese, he took out a notebook and began writing. The script was mostly foreign to me, but I made out the word *Toronto*, which he underlined. The two looked as if they came straight out of Hollywood casting, too real to be real. He listened to Victoria carefully, asked some more questions, and periodically would observe me as if to gauge whether I was to be taken seriously. Apparently I was. I felt as if I had fallen into a dream of Tibetan splendour—their faces seemed to glow.

"I speak some English," the young man said to me. "Your friend tell me you want to part from two spirits, an old woman and a young man. I need you to tell names."

"But I'm not the one that has seen them. Victoria has. I can only tell you who I think they might be."

"I will need their names."

I hesitated. Without waiting for my response, he wrote a series of numbers on a piece of paper, paused over one set and crossed them out, wrote some new numbers, and finally handed the paper over to Victoria. The bill! The payment schedule!

"Excuse me," I said, hoping that I was sounding respectful. "What will this exorcism cost? How much?"

"No money," he said, and barely concealed his smile. "But Madame Victoria will let you know what you do when you are back in Toronto. I must go to prayer and will return."

I stood up and shook his hand. He bowed to us and left the room. Victoria tugged at my sleeve.

"Let's visit upstairs," she said, "and ask the Goddess of Mercy to help you. I tell you what the student say you must do."

When we finished upstairs, the old lady was waiting to let us out. She handed me a bookmark laminated with a prayer and a picture of Kwan Yin, the Goddess of Mercy. A lucky red cord with two pearls dangled from it. Victoria laughed.

"I told him you are a writer of books," she said. "Use this for the Sunday ritual."

The ritual was going to take place in the temple hall with the Master conducting the ceremony—a monthly affair for the Vietnamese community. Victoria explained that I would not have to be present, but the Master would invoke the names of the two spirits. Could I write their names down? Yes, English lettering would do. The young man returned. I printed out Philip's full name and, since I never knew the name of my biological mother, I gave the other spirit the name Yook Mah Dahn—Jade Peony. I had Victoria explain the situation to the young man in Vietnamese, so that he could tell the Master. She did. He nodded sympathetically and said to me, "That be okay."

"No worry, Mr. Wayson," Victoria said, passing the slip of paper across the table.

Back in Toronto, adjusting for Eastern Standard Time, I was to meditate on the bookmark with Kwan Yin's image and tell the Goddess of Mercy to bless and guide the spirits back into the Other Side. The whole matter of a ceremony that I didn't believe in, to rid me of spirits that I couldn't see, left me feeling immensely sad. I wished I were someone like Victoria, so hard working in the real world, whose core strength was reinforced by her spiritual world.

I resisted being drawn into that world of hers. I still clung to the idea that she was being scammed in some way, that I had to rescue her from being duped. Maybe the numbers the young man had written down were the instalments she had to pay on my behalf.

On the ride back to the Mekong, Victoria handed over that piece of paper. Taking her eye off the road, she pointed out the schedule for the ceremony: the numbers for the month, day, and the matching time for Vancouver and Toronto. All numbers. She could not stop smiling. I wondered who was saving whom.

⌒

Later that afternoon, sitting in the living room, Larry removed his glasses, rubbed his eyes, and inclined his head towards me. I reported what had taken place, told him that the young monk-in-training was Philip's age, had the same build, the same eyes and high cheekbones.

"Well, Sonny." He hesitated, replacing his glasses and furrowing his brows. "You ever think of"—he hummed the "Twilight Zone" theme and deepened his voice—"*re-in-car-nation?*"

"That's stupid," I said, shocked at the longing piercing my heart, an aching for the impossible to be true—to have Philip back and alive. But seeing Larry doubled up with laughter, his fist pounding the sofa cushions, the spittle flying from his lips, I joined him in helpless laughter.

On my last day in Vancouver, Larry summoned me back to the Mekong. After leaving the temple days before, I had asked Victoria a final question that stumped her.

"Victoria," I began, cautiously, "I've been going to your restaurant for almost five years. How long have these two ghosts been with me?"

"What do you mean, Mr. Wayson?"

"Why haven't they shown up before now?"

Apparently, the famous Artemis had provided an answer Victoria was desperate to share. For my part, I had failed to uncover the great swindle; so far, I had not been asked for a single penny.

Without warning, just before I was to leave Jake and Alice's for the restaurant, nature struck. The house shook with a loud bang.

A storm cloud swallowed the sun and the whole kitchen darkened; a roar of hail plummeted down, bouncing off rooftops and rolling to the ground like tossed marbles. A few seconds of glass-rattling thunder, then nothing more. The sun came out. The house stood silent. Looking outside, I saw the last hailstones tumbling on the back porch. I hurried out of the house to meet with Victoria.

I knocked at the front windows of the Mekong, rubbing the wet pane so I could peer inside to see if Victoria was in the back. I saw her looking as if she had just collapsed in one of the chairs. She pushed herself up, rushed to the front, and unlocked the door.

"Mr. Wayson," she said, grabbing at my arm. She hurried me to the back table. "Did you hear that? The lightning? The thunder?"

"Yes, but are you okay?" I sat her down and pulled a chair up beside her.

"No, no," she said. She was clearly flustered. "You hear all that?"

"Calm down, Victoria. Let's rest a moment, okay?"

She had been a refugee from the fighting in Vietnam: the hail pelting the car roof must have stunned her. She bit her lips, but couldn't hold back.

"Artemis tell me to tell you that they come back with you."

"Come back? Who? I don't understand, Victoria."

"You ask how long they with you."

It was my turn to be surprised.

"Artemis say the two ghosts come back with you. She told me you die and come back with them. Did you know that?"

"No," I said. I wanted to say, *Not possible*, but instead I swallowed the words.

Someone opened the back door and came in—the cook arriving to prepare the kitchen and begin the day. Colour returned to Victoria's cheeks. Sunlight poured through the front French windows. I asked her to thank Artemis again, and we both stood up to say goodbye.

"You be careful, Mr. Wayson. You come back safe. No wheelchair."

I gave a little laugh, and we hugged each other.

On my flight home, I gripped the armrest, thought about my ghosts, and wondered if death might not be the end.

In Toronto I did cooperate with the prayer rituals scheduled for those two spirits in that Vancouver temple. In my attic room, I spoke to the image of Kwan Yin and asked for her assistance. Fearful that incense might trigger an asthma attack, I lit three candles, as Victoria had recommended. I urged the two ghosts to go back; I heard myself tell them that I would soon join them. As the candles flickered, I thought of the child who had been raised by a community of haunted storytellers. I felt neither foolish nor very much a hypocrite for following through with that calming hour. Instead, I felt respectful of something I couldn't quite explain.

I wet my thumb and two fingers and snuffed out each candle. I still do not believe in ghosts, but I confess that I talk to them. I write about them. They haunt me. I will not let them go.

That November, I flew across the ocean to Siena and enjoyed ten days of teaching in a fabled setting. Every morning from my hotel window, I would look out on San Gimignano with its crumbling watchtowers, the Tuscan hills with vineyards peeking through mist. After classes, I explored candlelit altars, cathedrals whose holy relics and stone foundations were older than sorrow. I roamed cobbled roads and narrow dirt lanes that curved between the high walls of courtyards and deserted piazzas. I found deeply inscribed on a stone tablet a fragment of the conclusion of Dante's *Divine Comedy:* "Love that moves the sun, the moon, and the other stars."

I returned home from Siena, suitcases stuffed with gifts and Italian stationery, and pushed my way through the airport crowds. Standing on my own two feet, I hailed a cab. No wheelchair required. At least, I thought, *not yet.*

Chapter 15

⁓

AFTER MUCH MENTAL TURMOIL, ENDLESSLY REWRITING chapter after chapter of *All That Matters*, the novel was finally completed. Concerns and questions about the meaning of family, of love, and of ghostly presences suffused the final draft, as if what I had been through over the last couple of years was now an essential part of the writing.

"I could have missed it all," I said to myself when the last page was done.

All That Matters was published just in time to be considered for the prestigious Giller Prize in 2004, and was awarded a place on the shortlist.

I was at home, standing by the kitchen counter, when the phone rang with the news. I had just turned over, quite randomly, a section of *The Globe and Mail* and seen a half-page picture of the author of *Bonjour Tristesse*, Françoise Sagan. *A sign.* I stared in disbelief at a youthful fawn-like face looking back at me, and the words, *Françoise Sagan . . . Author . . . Dead, at 69.*

Her high cheekbones were as sculptured as I remembered

them when I first beheld her leopard-skin coat in that spread in *Life* magazine. At seventeen, she had written a 125-page novel. By twenty-one, with her first book an international sensation, she stood resolutely beside her reward, her writing hand resting on the fender of her fiery red Jaguar.

Signs. Half a century ago, gazing at that picture when I was fifteen in Miss Shantz's Grade Ten English class in Quinte Secondary School in Belleville, Ontario, the son of parents running their first fish-and-chip restaurant on the Footbridge, I had said to myself, *I want to be a writer.*

At the gala for the prize, held in one of the plush banquet rooms of the Four Seasons Hotel in Yorkville, Mary Jo and my editor Martha sat to the right and left of me, lovely in their formal dresses. At the end of the evening, we stood up together to join in the joyful and thunderous ovation for the winner: "Alice Munro! For *Runaway!*"

Even more important than all the good or bad reviews to come, more important than winning or losing any prize, the nomination snapped me back to my senses: *I can write.*

All That Matters hit the bestseller list that fall. With great excitement, I headed into a publicity tour that lasted into the summer of 2005.

I didn't look behind. I didn't listen to those telling me that I should *rest up, get some more sleep, take it easy, slow down, take some real time off.* There was so much to do—and I had just signed a two-book contract, as the publicity put it, "for six figures"—and I wanted to keep going.

I tried to ignore my breathing, which became heavy and raspy. My lungs tightened. I could feel my heartbeat like a drum whenever I forgot my medication. I had recently crossed the borderline and was now a confirmed Type 2 diabetic. But still I was working with Rami, though our sessions were frequently interrupted; one, then two or three weeks of workouts were cancelled by my busy schedule. I demanded more exercises to make up for the missed sessions. My chest would pound, but I attributed that to the excitement of keeping up with Rami, and said nothing to him. I was simply tired.

Besides, I never felt any pain. If I held my breath for five seconds, if I rested on a bench for a few minutes and used the inhaler, I felt fine. *Pollen . . . allergies . . .* An extra puff and I *could* breathe easily again.

⌒

By September 2005, my room was once again crowded with mounds of research notes, my growing collections, the floor piled with books that I was tripping over, the boxes of clothes I had planned to unpack ready for the fall chill, everything scattered about demanding attention—I just wanted to get away for a month. I called up the only person who ever organized my things as if he actually enjoyed the challenge. Ken said he would straighten out the mess if I left him a key to the house.

But where would I go?

I thought of Françoise Sagan, in her tiny student room, tapping away on her typewriter, the leopard-skin coat tossed across the floor like a rug, and the double shutters flung wide open to the sound of Paris traffic. Why not the romantic equivalent for *moi?* Hadn't I been too busy with readings and charities? Didn't I deserve a break from this muggy town and my piles of stuff?

Out of the blue, Patrick, the director of photography from the Confucius film, called. He had kept in touch with me for the last two years from his home in Calgary, but we never managed to meet when he was in Toronto.

"I'm staying in Montreal in this really neat place," he said, "and you suddenly came into my head. I think it's about time we got together. How about it?"

He told me of a vacant room in the house where he was staying. There was an antique desk, a double bed, and a window that overlooked rows of elegant wrought-iron balconies across a parkette. *Perfect.*

"Call this number in thirty minutes," he said. "I'll tell the land-lady you're interested. Her name's Danielle and she's a writer."

~⌐

The musical voice at the other end of the line was a bit curt when I asked if she might consider renting the room for a few weeks.

"I'm sorry, *non, non,* you *must* be sure the *necessity* is to pay a full month. *Yes?*"

"Very fine," I said.

"You will send me a cheque, yes?"

"Yes, and I'll include one of my books if you read English," I said. "Do you read English?"

"Yes, yes, but not too much," she said. "I will read, thank you."

When I arrived by train, three suitcases overloaded as usual with my paraphernalia of pens, rubber stamps, what-if and can't-do-without books, laptop and printer, and clothes and . . . I handed the burden over to the taxi driver. He read the address on the slip of paper and we drove helter-skelter through cobbled streets. The semi-detached home was discreetly located on a quiet back laneway near the intersection of busy Mont-Royal and St. Denis. I negotiated the flight of narrow wooden steps, and at the last one had to use my puffer. I rang the doorbell.

Danielle opened the first door, then a second, onto a clean, well-lit living room, pausing to let me survey the room for a few minutes: the paintings on the walls, plush chairs and sofa, gleaming hardwood floors. Danielle was taller than most women, and beautiful, a little like the young Maggie Smith. I shucked off my street shoes.

"Shall we see the room, yes?"

She picked up my computer case and led the way up the stairs. One by one I picked up my suitcases and thumped up behind her. We stood in the hallway. She went to the far door and opened it. A large silver-grey cat scampered out and dashed past me down the stairs.

"*Voilà!*"

I gasped. I had an acute allergy to certain kinds of cats. But before I could mention the problem, Danielle gestured for me to follow her in. She opened the one window in the room, and the late-summer breeze swept by the sheers; the flimsy curtains billowed wide and high, exposing the view. Perfect. My room was perfect, just as Patrick had described it to me. An old writing desk that had seen better days sat in front of the opened window, the frame just wide enough for one person, in case of fire, to climb through to the wrought-iron balcony. An old wooden chair sat humbly beside the desk, almost like the one Van Gogh had painted in his bedroom in Arles.

Though exhausted by the train trip from Toronto, and with just hauling my luggage up two flights of stairs, I felt a jolt of inspiration. I imagined myself tapping on my laptop writing perfect prose from dusk till dawn. Danielle smiled to see me so happy with the room.

"You will see the bathroom, yes?"

"*Oui, Madame,*" I said, nearly exhausting my French vocabulary. I was pretty sure that *Madame* was appropriate for a woman of her maturity. Was she thirty-something, forty? "I think I'll clean up, too."

"Of course, of course! Please call me Danielle, Mr. Shoi!"

"Call me Wayson," I said.

"Yes, Way-sen, of course, of course! I like so much the way your name look on the book cover—Way-sen Shoi! Patrick told me so much about you, Way-sen."

"And he told me you write poetry."

"*Oui, oui!* My poems will be publish in an important anthology very soon."

"Congratulations," I said. "Patrick said you read English very well."

"Oh, *non, non*—but just enough to understand." She gently pointed out my book on the hall table. "You will sign for me later—when we know each other more?"

I warmed to her more and more.

"And you, Way-sen, do you read French?"

"No," I confessed, immediately remembering that I had, with some shameless grovelling, barely passed my one and only French class in Grade Eleven.

"Still, yes, yes!" she laughed. "We get along!"

"Oh, Danielle," I began in earnest, as my eyes began to itch, "about that big cat—"

"Willy?" she said. "My one and only big, *big* friend? Ah, I see, you have an aller-gee?"

"No, not always," I said. "We have a cat, too. I've gotten used to her. But I can't have him come into my room, just in case."

"Of course, *never, never!* I tell Willy not to do that. You keep your door close, Way-sen. We all get along, yes?"

⁓

The Great Willy, on the rare occasion when he was inadvertently locked outside, came through my bedroom window in the middle of the night, his yellow eyes scanning me with an intensity I mistook for affection. Willy decided to sleep at the foot of my bed. I sniffed through the night. By day he stayed away from my room, even if I left the door wide open. As Danielle often said, shrugging her shoulders delicately, *Who can explain love?*

I told myself my nose and eyes would get used to Willy, that I had to stop spending so much time enjoying Danielle's company and taking so many naps. I was turning into a character from one of Michel Tremblay's plays: everything reminded me of my childhood. When Danielle played the soundtrack from a recent Spanish movie, I thought of Old Chinatown and the Cantonese opera. Voices rose and fell, violins sang, heels clicked and clattered, drums roared, and the orchestra broke into a passionate roar. My eyes closing, I saw Cantonese opera warriors swirling in their sequined costumes, breaking into a tango. I woke up startled. Danielle said that I was too tired, that it was time for me to go to bed.

Alone in my room, I remembered my reason for being here in this literary metropolis of Yves Beauchemin, Mordecai Richler, Marie-Claire Blais, and Leonard Cohen. I read again their Montreal passages to absorb their descriptive power, but there was no use lying to myself: I hadn't tapped out a single word on my trusty laptop. Hadn't been able to read more than two or three pages before falling asleep, morning, noon, or night.

The moments I spent with Danielle distracted me. Beyond talk of books, writers, plays, and movies, we dared to share intimate stories. Danielle was a risk taker, and our conversations gave back to me an illusion of youth: I had all the time in the world to finish any book I wanted to.

"How's the writing?" Patrick asked when he stepped into the house carrying his overnight bag and interrupted Danielle midway through a sentence. Once again, his friendly blue eyes captivated me.

"Great," I said. "I'm really inspired here."

"*Oui, oui,*" Danielle said. "Way-sen is writing all the time in his room with the door closed."

Willy stretched out on his back beside me, closed his eyes, and his paws reached out and crossed over, as if he were praying.

"See, Patrick?" Danielle's voice rose grandly. "Willy blesses Way-sen!"

Willy's praying for me, I thought. *He knows my mind has been drifting backwards, and that I haven't written a single word.*

When Nina finally arrived, cheerfully pushing through the front door and waking me up from my nap on the sofa, she greeted me like an old neighbour. She was Patrick's wife, and had flown in to spend a ten-day break from their Calgary production office with him. She looked as lovely as I had imagined her—dark eyes, petite, a classy young East Asian beauty. We gave each other an instant hug.

Frustrated with days and nights of facing a blank screen, I needed a break, too. I decided take up Patrick's request to spend one day with Nina, an expert shopper—"just window shopping"—while he was filming. One became many, and we often added an exquisite lunch in a small café along St. Laurent. Nina had a knack for finding beautiful things at bargain prices, especially in clothes and shoes, which she wore to perfection.

On my last day in Montreal, we found the store we had been searching for, in a discreet laneway running just off St. Denis.

"Please tell me what you would like to see," the woman at the counter said. She pointed to a fine collection of rings and bracelets shimmering in the afternoon light. Nina saw how taken I was with a bracelet crafted with the ferocious heads of two horned dragons hooked together. The clerk swiftly followed my eyes, reached into the cabinet, and put the weighty bracelet in my palm. The thing belonged to me.

"Dragons are one of my signs," I said. "They usually bring me luck."

Nina beamed at my delight. "Looks like two lucky dragons for the price of one."

I looked at the price marked on its dangling tag: a handsome piece of work, but not quite a bargain.

"I love dragons and butterflies," Nina exclaimed. She took out her credit card. "This is to thank you for the origami butterfly you gave Patrick in Qufu to pass on to me. Remember?" She took my arm and pushed up my sleeve. "Some things are meant," she said, smoothly locking the bracelet around my wrist. "Patrick and I wanted to get you something. This is from both of us, Wayson."

"But that's too much," I said. "I can't—"

She cut me off with a quick kiss on the cheek.

The saleswoman applauded: "*Très belle!*"

I loved the way the chunky coil of silver felt cool on my wrist, but I should have noticed: the open-mouthed dragons were locked together face to face, a sign, an explicit warning of interesting times ahead.

Epilogue

I WAS ON THE PHONE WITH SHARON, DR. DAVID'S RECEPTIONIST. I had left Montreal reluctantly three days before and returned home exhausted. Hearing my gasping, Sharon put the call through to her boss.

He asked me what was wrong. I started to tell him about my breathing, but I couldn't stop coughing long enough to finish the explanation.

"Can you get here right away." It was a command, not a request.

As soon as I arrived, Sharon buzzed David to come out into the waiting room. I didn't stop to sit down with the seven or eight others waiting their turn.

In his examination room, after a quick check with his stethoscope, a pause to shake his head so that I could see he was going to be very serious, David gently put his arm around my shoulder and bent his head down towards my ear.

"Wayson," he said, "I *don't* want you to panic, but you seem to be heading for a heart attack. Right now, you're experiencing unstable angina."

"No, no," I protested, waving my dragon-headed wrist. "I just need a stronger puffer. One of those new inhalers I read about in—" My deep coughing interrupted again. "My asthma, my lungs feel tight and—"

"*Wayson!* You're the writer, remember? *I'm* the doctor. You got that?"

I nodded.

"You're going to take this note over to emergency at St. Michael's."

At St. Mike's, I handed over the note. The nurse, without even a glance at my ID, rushed me through for an examination.

Karl was with me by then. Remembering the last time I was here, I asked him to call Marie, and Jean and Gary. The nurse tugged at my sleeve. "I'm going to be fine," I told Karl. He unhooked my silver bracelet; the horned heads looked at me and then disappeared into Karl's pocket. "It can't be that serious. I don't even feel anything. Look, the coughing seems to have stopped."

"Wayson," he said, barely paying attention to me, "you have to go with the nurse. *Right now.*"

I was taken through swinging doors into the examination area. Whoever led me by the hand stopped and began to unbutton my shirt. I started to help.

"Don't move, Mr. Choy."

"You know," I objected, "I just need a stronger inhaler, one of those newer—"

She yelled something I didn't quite catch. I was led into an isolation room, the only bed available. People were moaning to the left and right of me. A familiar antiseptic smell assailed my nostrils. A doctor instantly showed up to check my vital signs. The stethoscope felt cold on my chest. She shook her head and told me to get up on the gurney. As she helped me take off my shirt, she shouted out, "Code Blue! Code Blue!"

Absurdly, I stayed calm. Adrenalin must have kicked in to stop me from panicking. As if on a movie set, I fantasized that a Scottish missionary Gregory Peck or Dr. Rock Hudson would soon swing by and save me. The nurse came back and taped a band around my wrist where the bracelet had been. On firm instructions, I snorted nitroglycerine and waited for some sort of explosive reaction. Nothing, not even a buzz. By the fifth take, still *nada*. I was disappointed. But the doctor was apparently satisfied that whatever she heard through her scope was now acceptable.

"Can I go home now?" I asked.

"Not quite, Mr. Choy," she said. Her ebony face glowed. "Don't worry. We'll let your friend in the waiting room know you're going upstairs for some more tests."

"I feel fine," I repeated. All I needed was a stronger inhaler.

Then she said, as her eyes drilled into mine, "No, you'll need more serious attention. Do you feel any pain in your chest?" She started filling in some official sheet.

"Nothing," I said. "Just some tightness, like before."

"Are you diabetic?"

"Type 2," I said, but before she could explain why my answer clearly troubled her, she was called away. The attending nurse came over and read the instruction sheet the doctor had pinned to my gurney, matched up the name on the identity band she held with the name and numbers on the sheet. Another weightless strip of plastic curved over my naked wrist and was snapped together. An orderly unlocked the wheels and began to push me down a wide hallway.

"Just lay very still, Mr. Choy," he said. "Can you do that for me?"

I had seen this movie before: the hero, blinded by his own ego, believing himself invincible because he had escaped death before, is struck down by his own fatal indulgences: delicious rich foods, a crowded life of unmet deadlines and obligations, a messy room . . .

"Try not to shift or move, Mr. Choy," another voice said. "We'll be back for you in a few minutes. We'll be hooking you up to a monitor."

I was left in a quiet, empty room. To distract myself, I ran my thumb along the wristband. A clock ticked loudly. I had not much to do now except to lie still, to accept that I would have to stick around and eat hospital food again, meditate on mortality, and wait for things to blow over.

⁓

The next day, my friend Janet came to see me at the cardio care unit. Her pal, the nurse named Craig, was able to confirm that I would be given a local anaesthetic for some investigative procedure. I recognized the description. I had had an angioplasty before.

"Mr. Choy," Craig said, looking at the blood pressure monitor, "you're lucky, lucky that your heart didn't burst. Do you remember the doctor telling you that ninety-five percent of your main artery is blocked?"

I had been given some more medication in preparation for some surgery. I nodded drowsily into space.

"What comes next?" Janet asked.

I heard Craig's dramatic sigh. "Means this," he said. "He has to have a quadruple bypass. Tomorrow." He leaned over the rail at the side of my bed and smiled brightly. "Not to worry, Mr. Choy. Quads are not exactly common, but they're pretty safe these days."

Janet stood on the other side of the bed and lifted up the bound galley from Random House that I had been reading. She was going to help me write down a few words of praise. The front cover featured both an unusual title, given my circumstances, and, ironically, given my situation, a veined human heart dripping droplets of blood.

"What's that?" Craig asked, and read the title of the galley Janet held aloft. "*Bloodletting and Other Miraculous Cures.* Lord help us!"

As soon as I finished dictating my blurb to Janet, Craig stepped forward.

"Don't look now, Mr. Choy," he said, cheerfully raising a syringe in the air, "but I've got a little prick for you."

"What for?" I asked.

"You're going to have a quadruple bypass tomorrow morning. Remember?"

⁓

The next thing I know, my mind was coming through a fog of faces, and Marie was saying to me, "Wayson, just come out of this thing. You've done it before."

"You better." It was a strong voice, and I knew it belonged to my friend Betty. "You have to live long enough to clean out your room yourself."

"Gawd," said Karl. "That means he'll never die."

"Never," Gary said.

Everyone faked some laughter so that I might think they had no doubts about the outcome. My heart laughed with them.

"What's it all about, Tosh?" I asked my patient goddaughter, half in jest, as she stood beside my bed this second time around. She felt my forehead for fever—a nurse's habit, no doubt—and looked at my eyes to see how much the drugs had affected my waking moment. They had taken out some tubes that morning. My chest felt sore.

"I don't know what it all means," she said. "As a nurse, I get to see everything, all of it: birth, life, incredible suffering, dying, miraculous recoveries. Maybe we shouldn't ask so many questions. Does it matter to you whether there's some final answer?"

I felt the comfort of her touch and I closed my eyes. I recalled a moment when I sat in the big fabric chair on her patio in Tucson. I had bolted upright at the loud whirling, pumping sound growing louder and louder, so loud that in my confusion I didn't know whether it was coming from inside my chest or was in my ears. It had been a while since my last medical crisis, and this was exactly the pulsing sound that came back to me in flashbacks, though usually when I was half asleep. But I was wide awake this time. I clutched my chest, but felt no pain. Tosh had pushed aside the sliding glass doors and come out to the patio.

"What's wrong, Wayson?"

"I—Do you hear that sound, too?"

"Yes," she said. "Listen to me carefully. Turn your head very slowly to the right. Not too fast. Don't move too quickly."

I turned my head, and saw the pellet body of a hummingbird shooting backwards, then its blur of wings whirled and clicked, and the bird darted up and down.

Tosh pointed above my head.

I had somehow pushed my chair so that the back of it was directly below the feeder. The frantic bird was signalling me to move away from its territory. I shifted the chair a foot away. The bird gave something like a beeping cry and went back to its feeding.

Tosh and I sat together in silence. Over to her side, I saw a second hummingbird, buzzing at the sliding door, darting back and forth at its own reflection in the glass. Its breast reflected a burst of scarlet and orange. Finally, it shot forward and smacked into the glass and fell to the deck in a slump. I started to get up.

"Don't touch it," Tosh said. "It'll recover and then just fly away."

The tiny iridescent blob on the ground began to stir. It suddenly hopped up. The wings began a flicking movement. The wing tips dissolved into a frenzied blur; the tiny body impossibly lifted into the air like a rocket and shot backwards, then forwards, then up and down. Satisfied its internal compass was back in place, it shot up fearlessly past my head and poked its needle-like beak into the feeder, joining its less colourful mate. Life went on, as usual.

"They actually migrate over five hundred miles in the wintertime," Tosh commented, "all the way to Central America. Apparently they don't stop for rest."

"They must soar on wind currents," I said. "Lift those wings and just ride them. I'd figure that one out pretty quickly."

The drugs were making me drowsy again. My eyelids closed of their own will. How long had Tosh been with me this second time at St. Michael's? I knew it was she who had lifted the thin flannel blanket up to the stapled red scar on my chest where they had removed my heart, she who had held my hand between hers, knitted her fingers between mine, and gently squeezed for the longest moment before she whispered goodbye and went to catch the plane back to Arizona. I knew her leaving was the sign that I would be okay. That I would be the same person I was before almost dying, twice. That all my faults would remain completely intact.

That night, I felt as if I were soaring, gliding on some invisible current. With my eyes shut tight, I saw a pattern of hands brushing against hands, multiplying into the millions, gestures making no headlines, sounding no trumpets, yet knitting together countless reasons for frenetic hearts—like mine—to rest in peace against uncertainty.

ACKNOWLEDGEMENTS

First, my heartfelt appreciation to the staff and volunteers, the professionals, the nurses and therapists of St. Michael's and Bridgepoint hospitals in Toronto for their thoughtful and continuing care. Many thanks to Dr. Jerry Zownir and the intensive care team who saw me through those first life-and-death emergencies in 2001; also, equal thanks to Dr. David A. Latter and St. Michael's Cardiovascular Surgery Unit who saved my life in 2004. Appreciation to the Bridgepoint "5-West Team" who worked with Dr. Mendl Malkin: to Carol Blackman Weinberg, Robyn Langeraap and Jackie Mofs; to Judy Bonham, Dorothy Kawaguchi, Joanne Guy, Sez Laung, Ran Sun, Kimberly Thorpe, and their incomparable colleagues.

Thanks also to Dr. Duncan Stewart and Dr. Beth Abramson. And for their continuing care and treasured friendship, I thank Dr. Charmaine E. Lok, Dr. Rowena Ridout and, not least, thanks to Dr. David E. Greenberg and his "exceptional receptionist," my fellow writer, Sharon Fiennes Clinton.

For their invaluable advice and papers regarding technical and medical matters, I thank Dr. Denise Bowes, Dr. Liam Durcan, Dr. Helen Holtby; also to my friends Dr. Au, Dr. Norman Talsky, and my goddaughter Tosh Noseworthy. The latter's expertise as a nurse in the Cardiovascular and Medical ICU at the University Medical Center in Tucson, greatly benefited me in countless ways.

Thanks to Denise Bukowski and Maya Mavjee for initial support and encouragement. For their contributions during the early stages of my research,

I thank Mirella Cirfi, Nancy Delcol, Margaret Hart, Lloyd Peer, Ken Puley, Martha Sheppard, Doris Tallon, and Larry Wong. I am grateful to Wendy O'Brien for her own essay, *Telling Time: Literature, Temporality and Trauma*, in which she concluded, "If stories do no more than restore to us this sense of lost time, of a time outside of time, have they not done enough?"

For their help with specific chapters, and the most discerning advice regarding the ongoing drafts of this work, my appreciation to Angela Fina, Beth Kaplan, Mary Jo Morris, Wendy O'Brien, Kit Wilson-Pote, Janet Somerville, Betty Thiessen, and Jacob and Alice Zilber. Appreciation to copy editor Shawn Oakey, one of the best eyes in the business; any faults, however, stubbornly remain my own. Further, I am grateful for the encouragement and frank criticisms of my colleagues Joseph Kertes, Charlotte Empy, and especially to Antanas Sileika who shattered my writer's block when he said, "Memory is just another form of fiction." For tackling my files and papers and wrestling them into some working order, I thank Ken Dyba.

For sharing their experiences with signs and hauntings, I am grateful to Jan de Bruyn, the Rev. Glen Eagle, Gene and Jan Kiss, S. Lau, Daphne Marlett, the Venerable Ann McNeil, Victoria Pham, Caroline van Rooyen, Linda Williams, Theo Wyne, and Dennis Yandle. Thanks to the hospitality of Angela Fina and the North Carolina Penland School of Crafts for harbouring a writer; thanks for the family support in Vancouver from Jacob and Alice Zilber and my Aunt Mary Lowe and her family; and for my delightful writer's *pied a terre* in Stratford, heartfelt thanks to William Whitehead and Trevor Green.

Intimate friends and extended family members I trust will identify with key moments in this work and glimpse themselves. Though others may not appear fully in these pages, you were warmly appreciated for being there when I most needed your best wishes, your cards and flowers; Eyo's hand-drawn rainbow, and the Lockwoods' Sunday visits with the *New York Times*. Similarly, when I felt like entirely giving up on this book after my laptop crashed again, I thank Geoffrey Taylor, Director of Authors at Harbourfront Centre, for his call to Massachusetts— *Yes, a sign!*—informing me of my being awarded the Harbourfront Festival Prize. And for rescuing my lost files, *three* times, thanks to the Computer Hospital's Sil Ferrari.

Finally, I'm most grateful for the unstinting dedication and expertise given to me by my genius editor, Martha Kanya-Forstner.

A NOTE ABOUT THE TYPE

Not Yet is set in Centaur, designed originally for New York's Metropolitan Museum in 1914 then adapted for general use in 1929. While a so-called modern face, Centaur is modelled on letters cut by the fifteenth-century printer Nicolas Jenson. Its italic, originally named Arrighi, was designed in 1925 and is based on the work of Ludovico degli Arrighi, a Renaissance scribe. Centaur is considered among the finest, most elegant faces for book-length work.

BOOK DESIGN BY CS RICHARDSON